CITY SPOTS
ZURICH

Thomas Cook

D0680937

WHAT'S IN YOUR GUIDEBOOK?

Independent authors Impartial up-to-date information from our travel experts who meticulously source local knowledge.

Experience Thomas Cook's 165 years in the travel industry and guidebook publishing enriches every word with expertise you can trust.

Travel know-how Contributions by thousands of staff around the globe, each one living and breathing travel.

Editors Travel-publishing professionals, pulling everything together to craft a perfect blend of words, pictures, maps and design.

You, the traveller We deliver a practical, no-nonsense approach to information, geared to how you really use it.

CITYSPOTS
ZURICH

Teresa Fisher

Written by Teresa Fisher
Original photography by Teresa Fisher
Front cover photography (Grossmünster) © Alan Becker / Getty Images
Series design based on an original concept by Studio 183 Limited

Produced by Cambridge Publishing Management Limited
Company Registration No. 1450464 England
Project Editor: Ross Hilton
Layout: Paul Queripel
Maps: PC Graphics
Transport map: © Communicarta Limited

Published by Thomas Cook Publishing
A division of Thomas Cook Tour Operations Limited
Company Registration No. 1450464 England
PO Box 227, Unit 18, Coningsby Road
Peterborough PE3 8SB, United Kingdom
email: books@thomascook.com
www.thomascookpublishing.com
+ 44 (0) 1733 416477

ISBN: 978-1-84157-767-8

First edition © 2007 Thomas Cook Publishing
Text © 2007 Thomas Cook Publishing
Maps © 2007 Thomas Cook Publishing
Series/Project Editor: Kelly Anne Pipes
Production/DTP: Steven Collins

Printed and bound in Spain by GraphyCems

CONTENTS

SYMBOLS KEY

The following symbols are used throughout this book:

ⓐ address ☏ telephone ⓦ website address
🕓 opening times Ⓝ public transport connections ❶ important

The following symbols are used on the maps:

𝒊	information office	O	city
✈	airport	O	large town
✚	hospital	○	small town
🛡	police station	═	motorway
🚌	bus station	—	main road
🚆	railway station		minor road
✝	cathedral	—	railway
❶	numbers denote featured cafés & restaurants		

Hotels and restaurants are graded by approximate price as follows:

£ budget ££ mid-range £££ expensive

◗ *The twin spires of St Peterskirche*

Introduction

There's more to Switzerland's largest city than gold bars and chocolate bars. Zurich has been declared 'Europe's hottest city' by *Wallpaper* magazine. It's a classical city with a contemporary edge, preserving its architectural and cultural heritage yet surprising the world with the latest innovations in art and architecture, fashion, shopping and design.

● *The River Limmat cuts through the historic Altstadt*

Forget the old image of a characterless and cold-hearted financial city of buttoned-up businessmen working in ubiquitous grey bank offices; of secret investment files and precision timing. Of course, the streets are meticulously clean and everything runs like clockwork, but it is also a fun-loving, dynamic and thriving metropolis. It is large enough to offer world-class facilities, but small enough to retain its Swiss charm and 19th-century intimacy.

Most of Zurich's sights fall within a compact, walkable area either side of the Limmat river, which bisects the city centre. The ancient hilly Niederdorf district to the east is a veritable labyrinth of ancient, cobbled lanes brimming with trendy bars, cafés and quirky shops. To the west, the Altstadt (Old Town) contains many of the city's finest historic buildings, and broad, leafy Bahnhofstrasse counts among the world's most sophisticated shopping boulevards. The newly trendy former industrial quarter of Zurich West reflects the city's radical change in recent years, while the lake, with its beautiful grassy parks and lakeside promenades, is framed by majestic, snow-capped mountains.

Located at the heart of Europe, today's Zurich cleverly combines the trams and architecture of Vienna, the waterways of Amsterdam, the street café society of Paris and the cobbled old-town atmosphere of Stockholm into one delightful city. Although not the nation's political capital, this heady mix – together with a world-class art and music scene, the most luxurious shopping in Europe and the infectious *joie de vivre* of its people – demonstrates the city's position as Switzerland's spiritual centre.

When to go

SEASONS & CLIMATE

The city has four distinct seasons, each with its different appeal:

Spring (March–May) is a lovely time to visit, before the summer crowds, and when the sweet-scented blossoms of the lime trees on Bahnhofstrasse are in bloom. The weather is mild but it can be rainy.

Summer (June–August) is the perfect time to visit, when the weather is at its finest and sunniest, although the city is at its busiest. The average summer temperature is around 22°C (71°F) and rarely rises above 30°C (86°F), and the humidity level is pleasant. Don't forget your swimming costume as a dip in the Limmat river or the lake is always refreshing on warm days and balmy evenings.

● *Zürichers spill on to the streets during the summer*

Autumn (September–November) is another popular time to visit, with plenty of crisp, clear, sunny days. The city is quieter and there are often some excellent bargains in the shops.

During winter (December–February), as soon as the thermometer falls below 0°C (32°F), the city is covered with a sugar-like sprinkling of snow. It is a magical time to visit, with shop windows elaborately decorated for Christmas and fairy lights illuminating the streets. However, the temperature usually ranges from a chilly –2°C (28°F) to just 4°C (39°F) by day (and it's even colder at night), so wrap up warmly if you intend to go Christmas shopping.

ANNUAL EVENTS

Zurich's special events and celebrations attract visitors from all around the world.

February–March

The first major festival of the year is the wild **ZüriCarneval** during Lent, with parades, fancy-dress, street entertainment and fireworks in the Niederdorf. ⓦ www.zurichcarneval.ch

April

The spring festival of **Sechseläuten** (Six o'Clock Bells) marks the end of winter, when traditionally people would stop work at the sound of the 18.00 church bells rather than at nightfall. The first ringing of the season became a celebration of the arrival of spring. The highlight of this traditional spectacle starts (generally on the third Monday of the month) with a Procession of the Guilds (Zug der Zünfte) through the streets, involving around 7,000 participants, 500 horses, several music ensembles and carriages. At 18.00 sharp, the guildsmen gallop round a giant bonfire by the lake and set fire to the Böögg, a snowman-like figure made of straw and fireworks, who represents winter. It is said that the faster his head explodes, the better the summer will be.

June–July
The Zurich Festival is one of Europe's top festivals, with an extensive programme of opera, music, theatre and cultural exhibitions throughout the city. ⓦ www.zuercher-festspiele.ch

July–August
The open-air **cinema season** runs over the two months, on the banks of the lake and the Limmat. ⓦ www.orangecinema.ch

August
In mid-August, over a million party-goers take to the streets for the colourful techno **Street Parade**, with dancing day and night. Bigger than London's Notting Hill Carnival, it is Europe's largest annual street party. ⓦ www.streetparade.ch

Held during the second half of August, the open-air, lakeside **Theater Spektakel** is among Europe's leading contemporary performing arts festivals. ⓦ www.theaterspektakel.ch

September
The Knabenschiessen is one of the oldest and most unusual festivals; a shooting competition for teenagers on the Albisgütli, followed by the largest three-day fair in Switzerland.

November

Expovina is the world's biggest wine-tasting show. It takes place aboard 12 boats on the lake and is a wonderful opportunity to taste some little-known Swiss wines. Ⓦ www.expovina.ch

December

During **Advent**, there are plenty of Christmas concerts and the aromas of gingerbread and *glühwein* (a type of mulled wine) fill the air. (The one at the Hauptbahnhof is Europe's largest covered Christmas market.) One of the loveliest Christmas festivities is the Lichterschwimmen, when floating candles are launched from the Rathausbrücke into the river.

The new year is welcomed in with great revelry and dazzling fireworks by the lake at the nation's largest **New Year's Eve party**. Ⓦ www.silvesterzauber.ch

---

PUBLIC HOLIDAYS

Offices and stores are closed on the following national holidays (except at the Hauptbahnhof and the airport):

New Year's Day 1 January
New Year's celebrations 2 January
Good Friday April
Easter Monday April
Ascension Day May
Whit Monday June
Bundesfeier (Swiss National Day) 1 August
Christmas Day 25 December
Boxing Day 26 December

Dada

It may seem surprising that the outlandish, deliberately nonsensical Dada art movement was founded here in neutral, bourgeois Zurich. However, the city had long been a centre of artistic and liberal thought, attracting such scholars as Lenin, Jung, Joyce and Mann. Neutrality during World War I made

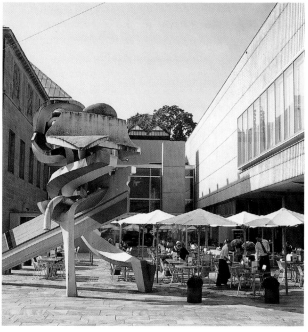

● *The Kunsthaus is home to seminal works of Dadaist art*

Zurich a refuge for dissidents, and so Dadaism was founded in 1916 at Cabaret Voltaire (❷ Spiegelgasse 1), a popular rendezvous for writers, painters and musicians. A rebellious anti-war movement and the very antithesis of conformity, it rejected the prevailing oppressive, materialistic standards in art by promoting a new 'anti-art'. The main exponents of the movement in Zurich included Hugo Ball, Tristan Tzara, Hans Arp and Emmy Hennings. Over the months, Dadaism gained support through public gatherings, discussion groups, readings and theatrical performances at Cabaret Voltaire. By 1920 the movement had reached its peak, and its influence reached beyond the visual and literary arts into 'Dada music', created by such composers as Erwin Schulhoff and Hans Heusser.

But Dadaism was not without its critics. A reviewer from the *American Art News* described it as 'the sickest, most paralyzing and most destructive thing that has ever originated from the brain of man'. Years later, even Dada artists described the movement as 'nihilistic... a phenomenon bursting forth in the midst of the post-war economic and moral crisis... a systematic work of destruction and demoralisation... embracing anarchy and the irrational'.

When World War I ended in 1918, many of the Zurich Dadaists returned to promote the movement in their home countries. Ironically, Dadaism went on to influence later, more positive art movements including Surrealism, Pop Art and Fluxus. Cabaret Voltaire fell into disrepair until it was occupied by a group claiming to be neo-Dadaists in 2002. After their eviction, the space reopened in 2004 as a museum dedicated to the history of Dada in Zurich.

History

Zurich's history dates back to 15 BC when a Roman customs post was established on the river on the site now called Lindenhof. They called it Turicum. The Romans built Zurich's first stone buildings and established a harbour and grapevines here. Around 250 people lived at Turicum, and you can see the remains of the ancient Roman baths through a metal grating in Thermengasse in the Altstadt. The Romans eventually withdrew from Zurich in 401 AD, to make way for the Franks and the Alemans. In 1218, Zurich was eventually recognized as a free city and was placed under the authority of the Holy Roman Emperor. To celebrate, the people of Zurich destroyed the Carolingian castle, using it as a quarry, and built the city's first Rathaus (town hall) on the banks of the Limmat river.

In 1336, nobleman Rudolf Brun, with the help of local craftsmen, ousted the city council from the Rathaus and founded the Constitution of the Guilds, thereby giving the city's artisans and traders economic and political power for several centuries. Brun made himself mayor and, during his rule, Zurich joined the Swiss Confederation in 1351 as the capital city of the canton of Zurich. The guilds remain active in society today.

During the Middle Ages, the Fraumünster was built as a convent for noblewomen, and the abbess was granted the right to hold markets, collect tolls and mint money. The Grossmünster was constructed, according to legend, by Charlemagne on the spot where Zurich's patron saints, the martyrs Felix and Regula, were buried (see page 82). Huldrych Zwingli, the first priest at the Grossmünster, initiated the Reformation from here in 1519.

His motto 'pray and work' was to have a profound effect on Zurich. In the second half of the 19th century, Alfred Escher, a trailblazer of modern Switzerland, built the Hauptbahnhof (main railway station) and founded the Swiss rail network, which revolutionized communications and made Zurich the nation's main transportation, research and business hub. It remained the country's political capital until 1848, when that honour was transferred to Bern.

Today Zurich remains the Swiss economic capital (half of the nation's income is generated here) and a major international financial centre. Many of the major Swiss banks have their headquarters here and it is home to the world's fourth-ranked stock market (after New York, Tokyo and London) and the largest gold bullion market. Combine this wealth and business prowess with a strong artistic and intellectual tradition, and a recent boom in gastronomy, dance clubs and popular culture… It is not surprising that Zurich is considered to be one of the most stylish cities in Europe.

◗ *View over the rooftops of historic Zurich*

Lifestyle

Ever since the 1980s, when the Wohlgroth community squat gained notoriety by erecting a huge imitation railway station sign to greet inbound trains to the Hauptbahnhof, which read 'Zu Reich' ('too rich') rather than 'Zurich', people have been joking about the city's affluent lifestyle. But it *is* one of Europe's most expensive cities. The streets are not lined with gold, but there's plenty of it in the city vaults and, of the million or so people living in the canton of Zurich, a disproportionate number are millionaires.

Zurich is Switzerland's largest city, spread across 93 sq km (36 sq miles), and the city itself has a population of around 330,000. This has declined recently as more young people choose to live in the countryside and commute to work. Only 6 per cent of Zürichers live in their own homes. The rest live in rented accommodation, as is the trend throughout Switzerland. Zurich is an important university city, with over 30,000 students in town, and foreigners have increased in recent years, now representing a quarter of the population. This has also resulted in greater religious freedom. Most Zürichers speak a form of German called *Schwyzerdütch* (Schweizer-Deutsch in standard German), with its own unique vocabulary, grammar and syntax.

Many Swiss stereotypes reign supreme here: everything runs like clockwork; everyone eats copious amounts of cheese and chocolate; the infamous 'gnomes' (as the British like to call Zurich's bankers) abound; and its citizens are generally law-abiding, efficient, hard-working, clean-living, polite and welcoming to visitors. Indeed, Zurich's hospitality is second to none, and 75 per cent of employees work in the service sector. But in recent years the laws have relaxed and so have the Zürichers. They work hard but they also play hard. The UK's *Guardian* newspaper recently described the Swiss as 'probably the most fortunate people on the planet. Healthy, wealthy, and, thanks to an outstanding education system, wise. They enjoy a life most of us can only dream about.' It therefore comes as no surprise that, for five years running, Switzerland's 'little big city' has been voted the world's number one place to live for quality of life.

● *Despite their reputation Zürichers know how to relax*

Culture

For centuries, Zurich has had a strong artistic and intellectual tradition. It has long been a centre of liberal thought, attracting such scholars as Joyce, Mann, Jung, Lenin and Wagner. In 1916 the avant-garde Dadaist movement (see pages 14–15) was born in the Niederdorf when a group of intellectuals rebelled against traditional artistic expression. Ever since, Zurich has been one of the global hubs of contemporary art, along with New York and London, and boasts more than 100 art galleries. Artistic excellence is maintained at the Kunsthaus, the city's foremost gallery, with its impressive collection of paintings and sculptures by Swiss and international masters, predominantly from the 19th and 20th centuries. The Migros Museum of Contemporary Art keeps abreast of the very latest trends, while the reopening of Cabaret Voltaire in 2004 marked the start of a brand new Dada era.

Zurich is also home to the largest number of museums in Switzerland and has more than 50 attractions revealing every aspect of Züricher history and lifestyle, from toys to tourism. However, none provides better insight into local life than the Schweizerisches Landesmuseum (Swiss National Museum) with its remarkable and extensive collections spanning pre-history and the present day.

Visitors can enjoy concerts and music festivals throughout the year, ranging from small-scale open-air concerts to blockbuster pop concerts at the Hallenstadion. Opera is world-class, with performances from September to May in

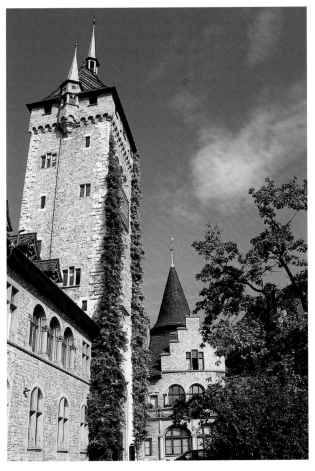

⬥ *The Schweizerisches Landesmuseum charts the history of the Swiss people*

the celebrated Opernhaus. During summer months the lakeside open-air cinema is always hugely popular.

Zurich is also undergoing a subcultural revolution, largely due to the re-invention of the formerly industrialised Züri-West district. New life has taken root within the old factory buildings, which now house a wide variety of hip bars and nightclubs. Best-known is the trendy Schiffbau, an alternative venue for Zurich's main theatre. And the world-renowned techno Street Parade (see page 12), with 24-hour dancing in the streets, is now Europe's largest annual street party.

Zurich wears its history on its sleeve through its eclectic mix of architecture, from the photogenic, ancient buildings of the Altstadt, painted in ice-cream shades, to the city's immaculately restored guildhalls flanking the Limmat river, which provide rare insights into bygone city life. Le Corbusier's pavilion by the shores of the lake has left a legacy of 20th-century innovation while, more recently, the converted industrial spaces of Züri-West are supreme examples of post-modern industrial architecture.

For an excellent cultural overview of the city, consider a guided cycle tour (ⓦ www.zurichbybike.ch) or, if you're really brave, a Ghost Walk (ⓦ www.ghostwalk.ch), which delves into the city's past history to find its 'ghosts, ghouls and things that go yodel in the night'!

● *Ornate dome of the Grossmünster*

Shopping

From beautifully hand-crafted Swiss-made articles through to international luxury labels, shopping in Zurich inspires the fashion-conscious, delights lovers of tradition and never fails to excite souvenir hunters.

The main shopping district occupies a square kilometre at the heart of the city. This area contains everything, from Switzerland's most sophisticated department stores, tiny boutiques and quirky specialist stores to the haute couture of the world-famous shopping mile, the Bahnhofstrasse. While the vaults of gold that power Switzerland's financial centre lie beneath Bahnhofstrasse, at street level the affluent, fur-clad locals are happy to admire the opulent window displays and splash out on the designer clothes, watches, jewellery and chocolates of Zurich's most celebrated boutiques.

The 'in' districts of Sihl and Zurich West specialise in small, trend-setting boutiques, selling everything imaginable whether you're after interior design prototypes or funky skirts for men. Niederdorf contains a multitude of interior design shops and galleries, while the artisan quarter at Schipfe offers treasure troves of antiquities. The city enjoys a flourishing art trade, especially along the Rämistrasse 'art mile'.

Not only does Zurich offer stylish international brand names, it also presents its own urban labels, including Freitag bags (made from recycled truck tarpaulins), street-, beach- and snow-wear with urban attitude from Alprausch, effortlessly fashionable designer shirts by local designer Edo Popken, and sumptuous silk accessories at Fabric Frontline. There is also a

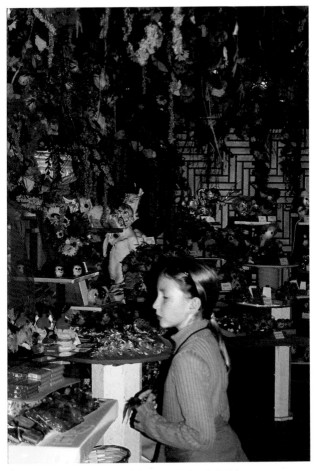

🔺 *Chocolate lovers will feel like kids in a sweet shop in Zurich*

bewildering choice of Swiss-made skis and snowboards, jewellery and watches. The finest local handicrafts can be found at Schweizer Heimatwerk. Failing that, there are plenty of nostalgic souvenir shops with amusing collections of beer steins, music boxes, Swiss knives, fondue pots, cuckoo clocks and cow bells...

Gourmands will enjoy the lavish international delicatessens at the Globus and Jelmoli department stores and the local fruit and vegetable market at Bürkliplatz on Tuesday and Friday morning (which becomes a flea market on Saturdays). And don't even think of leaving Zurich without buying some chocolate, as it is *the* speciality here. It's hard to miss such celebrated chocolate shops as Sprüngli and Teuscher, with their mouth-watering window displays. Cheese is perhaps Switzerland's most famous export, and several specialist cheese shops offer everything from delicious mountain goats' cheeses to the runniest of *raclette* cheeses.

USEFUL SHOPPING PHRASES

What time do the shops open/close?
Um wieviel Uhr öffnen/schließen die Geschäfte?
Oom veefeel oor erffnen/shleessen dee geshefter?

How much is this?
Wieviel kostet das?
Veefeel kostet das?

Can I try this on?
Kann ich das anprobieren?
Can ikh das anprobeeren?

Eating & drinking

The food scene in Zurich has never been as exciting as it is now, with trendy eateries and world-class restaurants burgeoning throughout the city. There are now nearly 2,000 bars, cafés and restaurants serving a bewildering range of culinary delicacies from around the world, and a remarkable 400 of these serve guests outdoors in mild weather.

Whatever your taste and budget, Zurich has just the right eatery for you, from noodle bars, sausage stands and beer cellars to innovative gourmet temples inside former factory walls, lakeside fish restaurants and traditional guildhall restaurants serving delicious Zurich specialities. Undoubtedly the most unusual dining experience is at Blinde Kuh (see page 91), the first restaurant in the world to be run by blind people, where you eat in total darkness. For a special occasion, Petermann's Kunststuben (see page 114) in nearby Küsnacht is Switzerland's top restaurant.

LOCAL SPECIALITIES

Traditional Swiss food is simple and hearty, relying heavily on dairy produce, and includes such humble mountain cuisine as

PRICE RATING
The ratings used in this book indicate the typical cost of a three-course meal for one person without drinks.
£ under CHF 25   ££ CHF 25–CHF 75   £££ over CHF 75

rösti (crispy, fried, grated potato), cheese and meat fondues, *Älpler Magrone* (macaroni cheese served with bacon, onions, puréed apples and cinnamon) and *raclette* (melted cheese piled high on new potatoes, gherkins and pickled onions). The neighbouring countries of Austria, Germany, Italy and France have also influenced the local cooking, which in Zurich is frequently meat-heavy due to its proximity to Germany. And recently other world cuisines have gained a foothold, with fusion cuisine all the rage in the city's more fashionable restaurants. Vegetarian restaurants are also on the increase.

Zurich's culinary identity comes largely from its location on Lake Zurich. Its cuisine mixes typical country specialities with some excellent fish dishes too, including such delicacies as lake trout, bream, perch and anglerfish. The city's signature dish,

● *Backstreet café in Niederdorf*

however, is *Züri Gschnetzlets* (Swiss-German for *geschnetzeltes Kalbfleisch nach Zürcherart*, veal in a cream and mushroom sauce). Look out also for *Leberknodli* (liver dumplings), potato croquettes, *Apfelkuechli* (fried apple slices), *Birchermüsli* (a delicious muesli, fruit and yoghurt mixture, generally eaten as a daytime snack or a light supper) and the ubiquitous *Apfelstrudel* (apple strudel), all commonplace on Züricher menus.

Fine dining and fine wine go hand in hand in Zurich and there is no shortage of excellent Swiss wine to try. The nation's best come from Valais and include *Fendant* (dry white) and *Dôle* (a smooth red). Zurich's vineyards are located mainly on the 'Gold Coast' of the lake's eastern shore. Look out for *Räuschling*, produced with exclusively Züricher grapes, and local *Schiterberger* and *Gamaret* reds. For spirits, try *Schnapps*, *Kirch*

EATING OUT

Eating out is very popular in Zurich and so it is advisable to make a reservation. In cafés, tea rooms, beer halls and less expensive restaurants, table sharing is common. Food is typically served 12.00–14.00 and 18.00–21.00 (22.00 at weekends).

By law restaurants have to display their menus and prices outside, so the price you see is the price you pay (it already includes a service charge of 15 per cent), and tipping is therefore not normally necessary. However, locals often round up the bill. The *Tagesmenu* (menu of the day), usually comprising two or even three courses, can be excellent value.

(cherry spirit), or *Xellent*, a new triple-distilled vodka made with high-quality Swiss rye and alpine glacier water.

PICNICKING

If a picnic lunch is more your style, make a beeline for the fabulous delicatessens in the basements of the Jelmoli and Globus department stores, the fruit and vegetable market at Bürkliplatz (Tuesday and Friday mornings), and local bakeries and cheese shops to stock up on provisions. The most popular picnic venue is the grassy lakeside but, for the energetic, the top of Uetliberg (Uetli Mountain) is undoubtedly the prime spot.

USEFUL DINING PHRASES

I would like a table for ... people
Ein Tisch für ... Personen, bitte
Ine teesh foor ... perzohnen, bitter

Waiter/waitress! may I have the bill, please?
Herr Ober/Fräulein, bitte!
Die Rechnung, bitte?
Hair ohber/froyline, bitter! Dee rekhnung, bitter?

I am a vegetarian. Does this contain meat?
Ich bin Vegetarier (Vegetarierin fem.).
Enthält das hier Fleisch?
Ish bin veggetaareer (veggetaareerin). Enthelt dass heer flyshe?

Where is the toilet (restroom) please?
Wo sind die Toiletten, bitte?
Voo zeent dee toletten, bitter?

Entertainment & nightlife

Forget yodelling, alp-horns and other types of traditional Swiss entertainment. Zurich is considerably less conservative than it was a decade ago and nights are now long and sophisticated with over 500 cool, stylish bars, clubs and discos to choose from, many in the Niederdorf and Züri-West quarters. Weekends begin on Thursdays and the city's flamboyant club scene caters to all tastes, although Latin, Techno and House beats take centre stage at present. That said, compared with people in other major European cities, most Zürichers are not night owls. Only a handful party till dawn, and many of the nightspots close down around 01.00 or 02.00 (later at weekends).

In the city centre, sophisticated chill-out bars draw the beautiful people, while most of the gay clubs and bars are located in the Niederdorf quarter, together with a handful of raucous beer cellars. This is also the most likely district to find buskers and other street performers. During summer, when the sun goes down things start to hot up at the city's pools and lidos, with their dreamy open-air bars idyllically located on the banks of the Limmat and the lakeside. The up-and-coming former industrial quarter of Züri-West has a special buzz about it, with its thriving subculture and its old factories converted into bars, clubs and leisure venues. The city also boasts numerous live music venues, ranging from mellow, intimate jazz bars and witty oom-pah bands in beer cellars to huge rock and pop arenas, featuring artists from all over the world.

On the cultural front, Zurich offers a prestigious programme of performing arts and cultural events throughout the year.

The main venue for classical music is the impressive Tonhalle with its superb acoustics, while the opera and ballet productions at the Opernhaus enjoy a world-wide reputation. Throughout the year, chamber concerts and recitals are staged in churches and museums, and in summer you'll find performances in some of the city parks.

The city's theatre programme is unlikely to appeal to visitors, unless you speak German, in which case there is the full spectrum on offer, from classical to avant-garde and even

⬤ *The Zurich Opera House hosts world-class productions*

puppet theatre for children (ⓦ www.theater-stadelhofen.ch). Cinema, however, is a different matter, with most screenings shown in the original version with subtitles. Open-air cinema is especially popular in summer, when giant screens are erected by the lake and river.

Tickets are best purchased from the relevant box office at each venue. Alternatively, you can book by phone or via the internet at www.ticketcorner.com, www.starticket.ch and www.tictec.ch. The cultural information desk of the Tourist Office in the Hauptbahnhof (ⓣ 044 215 40 00 ⓦ www.zuerich.com) offers advance bookings for theatre, musicals, opera, classical concerts, cabaret and other events, as do the department stores Jelmoli (ⓐ Seidengasse 1) and Migros (ⓐ Löwenstrasse 31), and BiZZ Central Ticket Office (ⓐ Bahnhofstrasse 9 ⓣ 044 221 22 83 ⓦ www.bizz-online.ch).

LISTINGS

The best source of local entertainment listings is the daily newspaper *Tages Anzeiger* (available from newsstands), whose weekly 'Züritipp' section previews cinema, theatre, music and nightlife. There are also listings in the daily *Neue Zürcherzeitung* (NZZ), while the monthly magazine *Swiss News* (available in newsagents and English bookshops) documents what's on in English. The Tourist Office is an excellent source of cultural knowledge, with its useful 'Zurich Events' leaflet, or pick up the nightlife booklets 'Wakeup Agenda' or 'Zurich Night Guide' in various bars around town.

Sport & relaxation

PARTICIPATION SPORTS

One of the joys of Zurich is its proximity to nature, with the river, the lake and the majestic mountains all on the doorstep. Zürichers enjoy a healthy outdoor lifestyle, including the following:

Boating

Hire a pedalo or a motorboat from various locations around the lake (see page 58).

Cycling

Throughout the summer season, Zürirollt offers free bike hire from stalls at the Hauptbahnhof, Globus-city and the Operahouse (for details see pages 104–105). ⓦ www.zuerirollt.ch

In-line skating

Tour the lake, and join the infamous Monday Night Skate (ⓐ departs from Bürkliplatz ⓦ www.nightskate.ch ⓛ every second Monday, spring–autumn) or the Swiss In-line Cup in June, the world's largest in-line marathon.

Swimming

Take a dip in the lake, the river or one of the many pools and lidos around the city (ⓦ www.badi-info.ch/zueri-badi.html). Alternatively, head to Alpamare (see page 108), the largest indoor water-park in Europe (ⓦ www.alpamare.ch).

Volleyball
There's beach volleyball during summer at the Flussbad Obere Letten lido.

Walking
Stroll along the lake, climb Uetliberg (see page 67) or hike in the wooded hills of the picture-postcard Zürcher Oberland region.

Winter sports
It takes just a couple of hours by train to reach some of the country's top ski resorts, such as Davos, Klosters, Flims and Laax. These are all easily accessible by train from the Hauptbahnhof (change in Landquart for Davos and Klosters; Chur for Flims and Laax), as are some smaller, lesser-known resorts, including Hoch Ybrig (see page 113) and Flums (change in Ziegelbrücke or Sargans), all within 1½ hours by train from Zurich.

● *The Zürichsee (Lake Zurich) is a great place to swim in the summer*

SPECTATOR SPORTS

Zurich's sporting events attract visitors from around the world. Many take place at the Hallenstadion (**w** www.hallenstadion.ch **N** S-Bahn: Bahnhof Oerlikon). Tickets are available from the box office or online at www.ticketcorner.com

Football

Zurich is the FIFA headquarters and occasionally hosts international football matches.

Freestyle.ch

An event showcasing all the latest tricks and stunts in snowboarding, free-skiing and skateboarding. **a** Landiwiese **w** www.freestyle.ch

Ice hockey

The Swiss team ZSC Lions plays at the Hallenstadion. Matches are played throughout the winter season and are always a thrill to watch. **a** Hallenstadion **w** www.zsc-lions.ch

Ice skating

Art on Ice is a glitzy show performed by international figure skaters in February. **a** Hallenstadion **w** www.artonice.ch

Marathon

The international Zurich Marathon, the largest in Switzerland, runs in April. **w** www.zurichmarathon.com

Accommodation

Swiss hospitality is world-renowned and Zurich has over 120 hotels ranging from 5-star deluxe and chic boutique hotels to simple guesthouses and youth hostels. Finding accommodation can be difficult, so try to reserve in advance.

As a general rule, the closer to the lake, the pricier the accommodation. The atmospheric Altstadt also commands high prices for its traditional ambience. More affordable hotels can be found in some of the backstreets, and especially in Niederdorf, although this quarter can be rather lively at night. Some of the cheapest accommodation is in trendy Zurich West.

City Backpacker £ A lively, international atmosphere greets you at this centrally placed youth hostel with private rooms, family rooms, dormitories and self-catering facilities.
ⓐ Niederdorfstrasse 5 ❶ 044 251 90 15
ⓦ www.city-backpacker.ch

Comfort Inn Royal £ Friendly, stylish business accommodation in the city centre. ⓐ Leonhardstrasse 6 ❶ 044 266 59 59
ⓦ www.comfortinn.ch

PRICE RATING
The ratings used in this book indicate the typical cost of a double room with breakfast for one night.
£ under CHF 250 ££ CHF 250–400 £££ over CHF 400

Hirschen £ This clean, simple, family-run guesthouse has been accommodating visitors at the heart of Niederdorf for more than 300 years. ⓐ Niederdorfstrasse 13 ⓣ 043 286 33 33 ⓦ www.hirschen-zuerich.ch

Leoneck £ An offbeat, fun choice, decorated in 'Swiss ethno' style. The rooms have original wall paintings by local artists, and there are cow motifs everywhere. Superb value. ⓐ Leonhardstrasse 1 ⓣ 044 254 22 22 ⓦ www.leoneck.ch

X-TRA £ At the heart of the trendy Züri-West district, this Bauhaus hotel adjoining the city's largest nightclub appeals to a young crowd. ⓐ Limmatstrasse 118 ⓣ 044 448 15 95 ⓦ www.x-tra.ch

Zürcherhof £ A popular business hotel with budget prices and non-smoking rooms, on the fringe of lively Niederdorf. ⓐ Zähringerstrasse 21 ⓣ 044 269 44 44 ⓦ www.hotelzuercherhof.ch

Greulich ££ A boutique hotel in a renovated industrial building, with minimalist furnishings and neutral colour schemes by Jean Pfaff, a Swiss artist known for his monochromatic art. The 18 rooms are clustered around inner courtyard gardens with birch trees and Zen-like water pools. ⓐ Herman Greulich-Strasse 56 ⓣ 043 243 42 42 ⓦ www.greulich.ch

Helmhaus ££ A friendly Niederdorf hotel combining traditional hospitality with modern comforts (including Wi-Fi throughout).

Ask for a room overlooking the river. ⓐ Schifflände 30
(am Limmatquai) ⓣ 044 251 88 10 ⓦ www.helmhaus.ch

Hôtel du Théâtre ££ Formerly a German-speaking theatre, this
stylish B&B near the Hauptbahnhof offers comfortable
accommodation with unusual theatrical decor. ⓐ Seilergraben
69 ⓣ 044 267 2670 ⓦ www.hotel-du-theatre.ch

Lady's First Design Hotel ££ This stucco-fronted 19th-century
villa near the lake once accommodated country girls at
finishing school. Today, its original features combine with chic,
21st-century decor. Facilities include a wellness centre (for
women only) and a fabulous roof terrace. ⓐ Mainaustrasse 24
ⓣ 044 380 80 10 ⓦ www.ladysfirst.ch ⓝ Tram: 4 (Feldeggstrasse)

⬥ City Backpacker is located in the heart of the city

Rigihof ££ A Bauhaus-style hotel near the university, with 66 rooms, each dedicated to celebrities once living or working in Zurich, including Max Bill, Carl Jung, Johanna Spyri, and many more. ⓐ Universitätstrasse 101 ⓣ 044 360 12 07 ⓦ www.hotel-rigihof.ch

Romantik Florhof ££ A romantic boutique hotel with just 35 rooms in a former 15th-century merchant's home, in a tranquil, leafy setting near the Kunsthaus. ⓐ Florhofgasse 4 ⓣ 044 250 26 26 ⓦ www.florhof.ch

Rössli ££ Ultra-small, stylish and affordable, this is a favourite with hip business travellers. Contemporary white-on-white decor and a charming roof terrace overlooking the old town. ⓐ Rössligasse 7 ⓣ 044 256 70 50 ⓦ www.hotelroessli.ch

Rutli ££ A simple, modern hotel at the heart of Niederdorf with unusual, graffiti-style decor. ⓐ Zähringerstrasse 43 ⓣ 044 254 58 00 ⓦ www.rutli.ch

Seefeld ££ State-of-the-art technology and design are the hallmarks of this trendy hotel, near the opera house, the lake and Bellevue. The bar draws the beautiful people of Zurich and there is also a roof terrace, Wi-Fi access throughout, and a small gym. ⓐ Seefeldstrasse 63 ⓣ 044 387 41 41 ⓦ www.hotel-seefeld.ch

Seidenhof ££ Just off Bahnhofstrasse, this highly functional yet stylish hotel was once an important centre for the city's silk trade. Facilities include Wi-Fi and high-speed internet access in all rooms, a minimalist, modern-Asian restaurant and a massage centre for its over-stressed business clientele. ⓐ Sihlstrasse 9 ⓣ 044 228 75 00 ⓦ www.seidenhof.ch; www.the-massage-therapy.ch

Uto Kulm ££–£££ For a truly tranquil retreat, escape the city bustle and stay in a car-free zone on Uetliberg, the 'Top of Zurich' (see page 67). Design is paramount in this classy, minimalist hotel, with its clever use of fine natural materials, and breathtaking vistas. For that special occasion, reserve a luxurious 'romantic' suite: the Tower Suite has a wood-burning stove and a heart-shaped whirlpool bath. ⓐ Uetliberg ⓣ 044 457 66 66 ⓦ www.utokulm.ch

Baur au Lac £££ Among Switzerland's grandest hotels, in an unsurpassed location adjoining Bahnhofstrasse and with a private park by the lake, this traditional, family-run hotel has welcomed such luminaries as Wagner, Liszt and Lennon since its opening in 1844. ⓐ Talstrasse 1 ⓣ 044 220 50 20 ⓦ www.bauraulac.ch

Widder £££ Just off Bahnhofstrasse, this striking, luxury hotel in the Altstadt consists of ten ancient interlinked townhouses, cleverly fused together by Zurich artist Tilla Theuss. Think ancient frescoes, exposed bricks and wooden beams brilliantly juxtaposed with glass and chrome, plus a roof-top terrace with spectacular views, and a chic jazz bar. ⓐ Rennweg 7 ⓣ 044 224 25 26 ⓦ www.widderhotel.ch

THE BEST OF ZURICH

Zurich is compact, and both easy and enjoyable to explore on foot, thanks to its beautiful lake, elegant streets, graceful spires and its maze of cobbled alleyways fringing the river. Most main sights lie in and around the car-free Altstadt and Niederdorf. The remainder are easily accessible by tram.

TOP 10 ATTRACTIONS

- **Schweizerisches Landesmuseum** Make this fascinating museum your first port of call. Once you have a grasp of the nation's colourful history, walks around town are all the more rewarding (see page 99).

- **Kunsthaus** Switzerland's top art gallery spans the centuries from the Middle Ages to the present, but specializes in 19th- and 20th-century Swiss art (see page 86).

- **Fraumünster** Famous for its five world-famous stained-glass windows by Chagall, which together represent a lavish fusion of colour and ethereality (see page 65).

- **Bahnhofstrasse** The city's main thoroughfare, a shoppers' paradise and the most overt manifestation of the country's wealth (see page 61).

- **Lake Zurich** An idyllic setting for boating, swimming, walking, picnicking or simply relaxing on the grassy banks (see pages 104–115).

- **Niederdorf** This ancient quarter, distinguished by its picturesque cobbled streets, tiny specialist shops, bars and restaurants, is especially atmospheric by night (see pages 78–93).

- **Grossmünster** The city's cathedral and the birthplace of the Swiss Reformation. Climb the tower for the best aerial views of the city (see page 79).

- **Altstadt** The city's most charming quarter, with its steep, cobbled lanes, beautiful mansions and tranquil, shady squares (see page 60).

- **Migros Museum für Gegenwartskunst** Extraordinary paintings, sculpture and photography by the top trend-setters in contemporary art, housed in a former brewery (see page 98).

- **Uetliberg** Affectionately called the 'Top of Zurich', Uetli Mountain has sensational 360° views of the city, the lake and the Alps (see page 67).

Ornamental beer steins

Here's a quick guide to seeing the best of Zurich, depending on the time you have available:

HALF-DAY: ZURICH IN A HURRY

If you only have a few hours, start at the Hauptbahnhof and stroll along the celebrated Bahnhofstrasse, admiring the glittering window displays. Stop for coffee at Sprüngli in Paradeplatz before heading down to the lake to glimpse the city's snow-capped, mountainous backdrop. Head back along the river to visit Fraumünster with its dazzling stained-glass windows by Chagall, or the Grossmünster on the east bank of the Limmat, before enjoying a snack in a typical Zurich café.

1 DAY: TIME TO SEE A LITTLE MORE

After you have completed the recommended half-day sightseeing, add a museum visit to your itinerary. The Schweizerisches Landesmuseum provides a fascinating historical background to the city, while the Kunsthaus is the city's finest gallery. Spend the rest of the day exploring Niederdorf, dipping into its delightful quirky boutiques, and its trendy cafés and bars, before enjoying a sumptuous dinner in one of the ancient guildhall restaurants.

2–3 DAYS: SHORT CITY-BREAK

The extra days provide plenty of time to explore the lake. Stroll along the east bank and take time out to watch the world go by. Then take a boat trip for a new perspective of the city. Alternatively, take in another museum – modern art lovers in particular will enjoy the Migros Museum – or climb to the summit of Uetliberg, Zurich's very own mountain. You'll also have time to eat some chocolate, buy some souvenirs, and check out the city's nightlife.

LONGER: ENJOYING ZURICH TO THE FULL

A longer stay enables you to soak up the café culture of Niederdorf, appreciate the relaxed yet efficient lifestyle of the Zürichers, and top up your tan in the city's legendry lidos. You should also take at least one trip out of town (see pages 104–126).

● *The Grossmünster dominates the Zurich skyline*

Something for nothing

Strapped for cash in one of the world's most expensive cities? Don't worry! There are plenty of sights and attractions to amuse you, without placing demands on your wallet.

Art aficionados on a budget need not be disappointed in Zurich, as many of the museums and galleries are free, including the Helmhaus (see page 85), the Museum Schweizer Hotellerie & Tourismus (Swiss Hostelry & Tourism Museum, see pages 86–87) and the Spielzeugmuseum (Toy Museum, see page 134). Even the beautiful Botanischer Garten, the pièce de résistance of all the city parks and gardens, is free (see page 78).

For a taste of historic Zurich, explore the Altstadt, where the hilly, cobbled streets are lined with romantic, shuttered houses, many painted in pastel shades and adorned with cascading geraniums. Don't forget to admire the interiors of the magnificent churches (most are free). Then soak up the atmosphere and people-watch in the sociable Niederdorf quarter (see pages 78–93). Better still, why not explore the city on a free hire bike (see page 34)?

Zurich is a shoppers' paradise and, even if you can't afford the shops' contents, you should certainly spend time admiring their window displays, particularly in the grand Bahnhofstrasse.

On a fine day, there is nothing more enjoyable than walking along the quaysides of the Limmat and the lake. The lake draws visitors and locals alike to its shores to relax, snooze, sunbathe or simply watch the world go by. In summer months, it's even warm enough for swimming. Stroll along its western shore and before long you'll be out in the countryside. Or, if you're feeling really energetic, climb to the top of Uetliberg for stunning views of the city and the Alps and a picnic spot to take your breath away.

If you're lucky, you may experience one of Zurich's 'free' street parties (see pages 11–12), should your visit coincide with one of the annual celebrations for Carnival, Sechseläuten or New Year, or the massive Street Parade in August.

Finally, who says everything in Switzerland is expensive? Zurich serves free drinks... from its 1,200 ornamental drinking fountains! They all provide free water to quench your thirst after a long, hot, 'free' day of sightseeing.

⬤ *The Helmhaus holds free exhibitions of cutting-edge art*

When it rains

The bad news is that it can rain in Zurich at any time of year. But the good news is that there are plenty of attractions catering for all ages and interests to keep you amused in the heaviest downpour or even in a winter snowstorm.

For starters, why not take a guided Classic Trolley Tour of the city? It's a great way to get your bearings, to learn a little about

● Hop on a Trolley for a whistle-stop tour of the city

the history and lifestyle of the Zürichers, and to sightsee under cover.

Avoid the showers by visiting one of over 50 museums and galleries catering for all ages and interests, from high-brow contemporary art to toy, chocolate and watch museums. At the Kunsthaus, Zurich's premier gallery, the sun-drenched Impressionist landscapes of Monet, Cézanne and Van Gogh are bound to brighten the rainiest of days. Or seek refuge from the elements in the city's magnificent churches. Fraumünster is best known for its stunning Chagall stained-glass windows, while Grossmünster, the city's cathedral, is austere but grandiose.

Zurich's shopping ranks among the best in the world, and there are several large department stores in and around Bahnhofstrasse (including Globus, Jemoli, Grieder and Manor) to occupy any keen shopper for hours.

Children young and old will love a visit to Zoo Zurich (see page 83) even in the rain; there are numerous indoor displays, which include a spectacular rainforest with its own tropical microclimate. Alpamare (see page 108), the largest covered aquatic park in Europe, with its massive tangle of slides, whirlpools and thermal pools, is also an ideal family outing when it's wet.

If that sounds too energetic, join locals for the fine Zurich tradition of coffee and cake mid-morning, mid-afternoon, or indeed at any time. Sprüngli at Paradeplatz or Café Schober in Niederdorf are two of the best-loved venues. And in the evening, take your pick of trendy designer bars, cosy, old-fashioned beer cellars, or intimate, candle-lit traditional bars.

On arrival

TIME DIFFERENCES

Zurich follows Central European Time (CET), which is one hour ahead of Greenwich Mean Time (GMT+1). During Daylight Saving Time (late Mar–late Sept), the clocks are put ahead one hour. At 12.00 in Zurich in summer, times elsewhere are as follows:

Australia Eastern Standard Time 20.00, Central Standard Time 19.30, Western Standard Time 18.00
New Zealand 22.00
South Africa 12.00
UK 11.00
USA & Canada Newfoundland Time 07.30, Atlantic Canada Time 07.00, Eastern Time 06.00, Central Time 05.00, Mountain Time 04.00, Pacific Time 03.00, Alaska 02.00

ARRIVING

By air

Zurich's Kloten Airport, Switzerland's largest international airport, has excellent facilities and shopping.
ⓦ www.zurich-airport.com

   The airport is located 11 km (7 miles) north of the city. The 24-hour taxi service to the city centre is expensive (around CHF 50). Alternatively, there is a train every 10 minutes to the Hauptbahnhof (main station), operating 06.00–24.00, which takes 10 minutes and costs CHF 5.80. Some hotels offer a direct airport shuttle service.

By rail

The swift, punctual Swiss railway network provides easy access to the city and enjoyable, stress-free excursions further afield. More than 1,900 trains halt at the Hauptbahnhof (main railway station) daily from all over Europe (ticket office ● 05.30–23.15 daily).

By road

Zurich's main bus station is located at Sihlquai (ⓐ Ausstellungsstrasse 15 ● 044 216 53 39), just behind the Hauptbahnhof. An efficient bus network connects all the main cities in Switzerland and abroad.

Driving in Switzerland is relatively straightforward and Zurich is easily accessed via the N1 motorway from Bern (to the west) or St Gallen (to the east).

⬤ The Hauptbahnhof, Zurich's main train station

> **DRIVING IN SWITZERLAND**
> Before you enter the country, you need to purchase a *vignette* (annual motorway tax), costing around CHF 27, available in advance from the Switzerland Travel Centre in London (☎ 0800 100 200 30 �🌐 www.swisstravelsystem.com) or on arrival in Switzerland from border customs offices, service stations, garages and post offices. Failure to display one on a motorway can result in a hefty fine.

FINDING YOUR FEET

There is no need to worry about your arrival in Zurich. Despite first impressions of an ultra-efficient, spick and span city, the pace of life here is surprisingly relaxed and the people are friendly and happy to help visitors. It is also a safe city with a low crime rate. However, there are incidents of petty crime, so it is advisable to take common-sense precautions (see 'Health, safety & crime', page 131), especially in Zurich West and at the northern end of Niederdorf.

ORIENTATION

It is easy to find your way around as the city is divided into districts, each with their own distinctive characteristics. Many quarters are pedestrianised, including Bahnhofstrasse, Zurich's most celebrated shopping boulevard. You may get lost in the labyrinth of narrow streets and alleys of the Altstadt (on the west bank of Limmat river) or Niederdorf (on the east bank), but that is half the fun. You can always arm yourself with a good map, but should you get lost, there are city maps at the tram stops, and a host of unmissable landmarks, such as the river, the lake, and the spires of the Grossmünster, Fraumünster and St-Peterskirche to help you get your bearings.

GETTING AROUND

Zurich's public transport system is operated by **VBZ Züri-Linie** (Zurich Public Transport ☎ 044 212 37 37 ⓦ www.vbz.ch). The ticket systems of all public transport in the canton are linked together, which means you only need one ticket whether you travel by tram, bus, boat or train.

By tram & bus

The extensive, efficient network of trams and buses runs daily from 05.30 to 00.30. You must buy a ticket before you embark, or you may be fined. Many different types of ticket are available, including a *Kurzstrecke*, valid for a trip of up to four stops, and a *Tageskarte*, which is valid for one day.

ZÜRICHCARD

If you are staying in the city for two or three days and plan to sightsee, consider getting a ZürichCard, which offers unlimited travel by tram, bus, train, boat, cable-car and funicular, free entry to over 40 museums, and a host of other attractive offers and discounts. 24 and 72 hour versions are available and can be purchased from VBZ ticket booths, train stations, the airport, major hotels and the Tourist Office in the Hauptbahnhof (main railway station). Remember, the ticket is only valid once you have stamped it in one of the ticket machines at a transport stop.

Buchegggplatz 15

Bahnhof Stettbach 7

9 Hirzenbach   Bahnhof Oerlikon 10

A Communicarta
Style45 design
© Communicarta Ltd 2006 UDN.1
Map user Ref:WZFG/CS/ZRH/2006/60/4

Röslistr.

Ottikerstr.

Sonneggstr.

Haldenegg

Langmauerstr.

Letzistr.

Kinkelstr.

Seilbahn Rigiblick

Winkelriedstr.

Haldenbach

Zoo 6

Susenbergstraße

Zürichbergstraße

Toblerplatz

Kirche Fluntern 5

Eth/
Universitätsspital

Voltastraße

Platte

Central

Neumarkt

Rudolf-
Brun-Brücke

Rathaus

Helmhaus

Kantonsschule

Kunsthaus

Hottingerplatz

Hölderlinstraße

Romerhof

Klusplatz

3 8 15

Englischviertelstr.

Bahnhof
Stadelhofen

Signaustr.

Bellevue

Kreuzplatz

Hegibachplatz

Hedwigsteig

Wetlistr.

Burgweis

Balgrist

Obernhaus

Kreuzstr.

Feldeggstr.

Höschgasse

Fröhlichstr.

Wildbachstr.

4 2 Bahnhof
Tiefenbrunnen

Friedhof
Enzenbühl

11 Rehalp

By bicycle

Zürirollt offers free bike hire from mid-May–Oct, from small white stands located outside the Hauptbahnhof, Globus-city and the Operahouse. ⏰ 07.30–21.20 May–Oct
ⓦ www.zuerirollt.ch

By boat

Zürichsee Schifffahrt (ⓦ www.zsg.ch) operates lake cruises from Bürkliplatz Pier throughout the year, as well as speciality cruises, which include a sunset cruise, a summer brunch boat and a winter fondue boat. **Limmatschifffahrt** (ⓦ www.zvv.ch) plies up Limmat river from Bürkliplatz Pier to the Landesmuseum twice an hour from Apr–Oct.

By car

There is little need for a car in Zurich, as the public transport system is so reliable and efficient. City centre parking is scarce and expensive.

CAR HIRE

It is only worthwhile hiring a car if you are heading out of town to explore the countryside. There are several hire car companies at the airport.

Avis ☏ 0848 81 18 18 ⓦ www.avis.ch
Budget ☏ 044 813 31 31 ⓦ www.budget.com
Europcar ☏ 043 255 56 56 ⓦ www.europcar.ch

▶ *The slender-spired Fraumünster*

Central Zurich

Central Zurich is the district of high finance and elegant shops, centred round the celebrated Bahnhofstrasse, one of Europe's most prestigious streets, where all Zürichers come to promenade and shop. Clinging to the banks of the Limmat river, the neighbouring, car-free Altstadt is the oldest part of town, with its delightful cobbled lanes and luxury boutiques. The entire district is dominated by its spires – the slender green spire of Fraumünster and the graceful spire of St-Peterskirche, featuring the largest clock face in Europe.

SIGHTS & ATTRACTIONS

Altstadt (Old Town)

The early medieval Old Town flanks the Limmat river and is characterized by a cobweb of picturesque lanes, steep cobbled alleyways and hidden sun-splashed squares. The streets are lined with romantic, ancient houses, many adorned with cascading geraniums. Highlights include: Lindenhof, the former Roman customs post; Weinplatz, the oldest market square; Thermengasse, an alley constructed over an excavated Roman bath; Augustinergasse, a street with attractive oriel windows; Münsterhof, the grandest square; and Münzplatz, overlooked by the Augustinerkirche, an austere but beautiful church that was secularized for a while during the Reformation for use as the town's mint.

Ⓝ Tram: 6, 7, 11, 13 (Rennweg); Tram: 2, 6, 7, 8, 9, 11, 13 (Paradeplatz)

Bahnhofstrasse

Bahnhofstrasse is reputed to have the most expensive real estate prices in the world. However, it is perhaps best known for its shopping. Indeed, this car-free shopping mile symbolises everything Zurich represents; elegance and prestige, quality, financial prowess and economic diversity. It leads from the Hauptbahnhof (main railway station) to Lake Zurich, and follows the ancient course of the western city wall, past some of the most exclusive jewellers, watchmakers and fashion boutiques in the world.

Two-thirds of the way along lies Paradeplatz (Parade Square), the scene of a medieval market until the 19th century, when it became the main venue for military processions. Nowadays it is the modern centre of the city, a major tram intersection, and the

● *A characteristic Altstadt house*

Central Zurich

0 — 250 metres
0 — 250 yards

**Map labels:**

WIENBERGGASSE WEG
SONNEGG STRASSE
UNIVERSITÄT STRASSE
BOLLEY STR
HÜTTEN STR
HOCHSTR
VOLTA STRASSE
GLADBACH STRASSE
CLAUSIUS STRASSE
LEONHARD STRASSE
AUF DER MAUER
SCHMELZBERG
STERNWALD STR
GLORIA STRASSE
GELLERT STR
KANT STR
TANNEN STR
SEILER GRABEN
HIRSCHENGRABEN
Hochschule Zurich Zentrun
E SCHMID STR
Universität Zurich Zentrun
KÜNSTLER GRABEN
SEMPERSTG
DR FAUST ST
RÄMISTRASSE
GLORIA STRASSE
MOUSSON STR
NÄGELISTR
PESTALOZ
ATTENHOFER STRASSE
SPIEGELHOF STRASSE
MÜHLE GASSE
ZÄHRINGER PLATZ
PFROGOR
NEUMANN
FLORHOF G
FLORHOF G
KANTONSSCHULSTR
ZÜRICHBERG STRASSE
PLATTEN STRASSE
ELEONOREN
STRASSE
SPIEGEL G
UNTERE ZAUNE
KIRCHGASSE
SEILER GRABEN
HIRSCHENGRABEN
Künsthaus
FREIESTRASSE
FREIESTRASSE
STRASSE
HOF STRASSE
DOLDER STRASSE
Grossmünster Cathedral
CÄCILIEN
STEINWEIS
WIEFRED STR
SCHÖNBÜHL
IGEN STRASSE
OBERDORF STRASSE
HOTTINGER
STRASSE
RÄMISTRASSE
PROMENADENG
ZELT
GEMÜNDE
KASINO STR
ENGLISCHVIERTEL
FREIESTRASSE
BELLEVUE PLATZ
DIGA STR
WEG
GASSE
MINERVA
MERKUR STRASSE
NEPLUN STRASSE
STADHOFER STRASSE
THEATER STR
SCHLECK STR
SCHANZEN
Zurich Stadelhofen
HOHENBÜHL STR
MERKUR STR
UTO QUAI
G KELLER
FALKEN STR
KREUZBÜHL STRASSE
MÜTERBACH STR
KLOSBACH
GOETHE
Opernhaus

Legend:

⛪	Cathedral
ℹ️	Information
🚓	Police Station
✈️	Airport
🚉	Railway Stn
🚌	Bus Station
➕	Hospital

N

main location of Sprüngli, the city's most celebrated confectioner. The bars and cafés here offer some of the best people-watching in town.

Bahnhofstrasse ends at Bürkliplatz, the main departure point for boat trips, with majestic views across the lake to the distant snow-capped mountains.

ⓐ Bahnhofstrasse ⓦ www.bahnhofstrasse-zuerich.ch ⓝ Tram: 6, 7, 11, 13 (Bahnhofstrasse); Tram: 2, 6, 7, 8, 9, 11, 13 (Paradeplatz); Tram: 2, 8, 9, 11 (Bürkliplatz)

Frauenbadi-Stadthausquai

This small, riverside lido is the only surviving example of a typical 19th-century floating lido and it provides an oasis of calm at the heart of the city, open only to women for swimming, massage and relaxation. By night, it becomes the Barfuss Bar, popular with both men and women, but everyone must be 'barefoot', as the name suggests.

ⓐ Stadthausquai ⓣ 044 211 95 92 ⓛ lido 07.30–19.30

A GOLDEN CITY

There's no denying the Swiss are an affluent nation and it's in Zurich that the serious money begins. Most major Swiss banks have their headquarters in and around Paradeplatz, and Zurich is the world's largest gold market. When you stroll up wealthy Bahnhofstrasse you're actually walking on gold. Admittedly, the street is not paved with it but, immediately beneath your feet, the massive bank vaults are full of gold ingots.

mid-May–mid-Sept (depending on water temperature)

 Tram: 2, 8, 9, 11 (Börsenstrasse). Admission charge

Fraumünster

The main attraction of this elegant church with its slim green spire is the five stained-glass chancel windows created by Marc Chagall in 1970. Each window has its own colour theme; the blue 'Jacob' window, the green 'Christ' window, and the yellow 'Zion' window are on the main wall, flanked by the red 'Prophets' window to the left and the blue 'Law' window to the right.

The church itself is situated beside the river, overlooking the picturesque old town square and former pig market, Münsterhof. The edifice dates from the 13th century, built on the site of an early Benedictine abbey whose crypt has been preserved beneath the church.

ⓐ Fraumünsterstrasse ⓒ 10.00–18.00 Mon–Sat, 11.15–18.00 Sun, Apr–Oct, 10.00–16.00 Mon–Sat, 11.15–16.00 Sun, Nov–Mar

Ⓝ Tram: 2, 6, 7, 8, 9, 11, 13 (Paradeplatz)

Limmat (Limmat River)

The city is bisected by the river, which flows from the northern end of Lake Zurich. Its most scenic stretch is from Bahnhofbrücke to Quaibrücke, where the attractive, multi-coloured houses of the historic old town flank both banks. Between these two bridges, four further crossing points (Muhlesteg, Rudolf-Brun-Brücke, Rathausbrücke and Münsterbrücke) unite the east and west banks of the city. The Schipfe, Wuhre and Stadthausquai are especially pleasant for strolling. During summer months cruise vessels ply the river between the Swiss National Museum and the lake.

Lindenhof

The bird's-eye views merit the steep climb to tranquil Lindenhof, the oldest part of Zurich and the original site of the Romans in 15 BC (see page 16). Today this broad, leafy square overlooking the roofs of the Altstadt is an oasis of peace, popular with locals for lunch breaks, and old-timers for *boules* and chess. The surrounding streets contain some of the city's most beautiful medieval wood-framed houses.

ⓐ Lindenhof Ⓝ Tram: 6, 7, 11, 13 (Rennweg)

St-Peterskirche (St Peter's Church)

No matter where you are in the city, it's hard to miss St Peter's, as it boasts the largest clock face in Europe, 8.7 m (28.5 ft) in diameter. The church itself is the city's oldest parish church, founded in the early 7th century, while the tranquil St Peterhofstatt is considered the Altstadt's loveliest square.

ⓞ *The Münsterbrücke links the east and west banks of the Limmat River*

ⓐ St Peterhofstatt ⓛ 08.00–18.00 Mon–Fri, 08.00–04.00 Sat
Ⓝ Tram: 6, 7, 11, 13 (Rennweg)

Uetliberg (Uetli Mountain)

Uetliberg is the tallest point in the city, at 871 m (2,857 ft). From here there is a popular two-hour hiking route along a forested mountain ridge, with glorious views over the city, the lake and the Alps. Just 15 minutes from the high-tech, jet-set glamour of the city centre, you can escape to the lush meadows, tinkling cowbells and chocolate-box landscapes that set Switzerland apart.
Ⓝ S-Bahn: Uetliberg Ⓦ www.uetliberg.ch

Zürichsee (Lake Zurich)

The 'blue lung' of the city and the fourth largest lake in Switzerland is hugely popular with Zürichers for boating, strolling, swimming, sunbathing, barbecuing or simply chilling out. No trip to Zurich is complete without a mini-cruise to admire the grandiose mansions lining the shores, and Bürkliplatz is the chief departure point for boat trips on the lake. Choose from a variety of year-round excursions ranging from nostalgic paddle-steamer tours to fondue cruises (see pages 104–115).

CULTURE

Haus Konstruktiv (House for Constructive Art)

The Constructive Art Movement was founded in Zurich. Leading exponents Max Bill, Verena Loewensberg, Camille

Graeser and Richard Paul Lohse all had their ateliers here, and their abstract art forms, based on geometric principles, came to the fore during World War II. Today, the Foundation for Constructive Art is housed in a former power station on the Sihl river, close to the city centre, and hosts regular temporary exhibitions to promote Constructivist, Concrete and Concept art and design.

ⓐ ewz-Unterwerk Selnau, Selnaustrasse 25 ⓣ 044 217 70 80 ⓦ www.hauskonstruktiv.ch ⓛ 12.00–18.00 Tues, Thur–Fri, 12.00–20.00 Wed, 11.00–18.00 Sat&Sun ⓥ Tram: 8 (Bahnhof Selnau); Tram: 2, 3, 9, 14 (Stauffacher). Admission charge

Museum Bärengasse

The Bärengasse Museum forms part of the Swiss National Museum. Housed in two beautiful baroque houses, it provides a rare insight into Renaissance city life through an appealing collection of furnishings, costumes, coins, musical instruments, maps and portraits of local dignitaries. There is also a small doll museum.

ⓐ Bärengasse 20–22 ⓣ 044 211 17 16 ⓦ www.musee-suisse.ch/baerengasse ⓛ 10.30–17.00 Tues–Sun, Jan–Feb; 14.00–20.00 Tues, 14.00–18.00 Wed–Sun, Mar–Dec ⓥ Tram: 2, 6, 7, 8, 9, 11, 13 (Paradeplatz). Admission charge

Museum Rietberg

Set in lush parkland, the Rietberg Museum is Switzerland's only gallery for non-European cultures, and boasts an internationally renowned collection of art from Asia, Africa, America and Oceania. The core of the collection was donated to the city by

Baron Eduard von der Heydt in 1952. Highlights can be seen in the magnificent neoclassical Villa Wesendonck, with ancient Oriental, Islamic and Indian painting and artefacts displayed in Villa Rieter. A new extension is due to open February 2007.

ⓐ Gablerstrasse 15 ⓣ 044 206 31 31 ⓦ www.rietberg.ch
🕒 10.00–17.00 Tues–Sun (until 20.00 Wed), Apr–Sept;
10.00–17.00 Tues–Sun, Oct–Mar ⓝ Tram: 7 (Museum Rietberg).
Admission charge

Uhrenmuseum Beyer Zurich
(Clock & Watch Museum Beyer Zurich)

This small but fascinating museum in the basement of the celebrated Beyer Chronometrie store contains over 500 time-pieces ranging from wooden-wheel clocks, water clocks, sundials and traditional cuckoo-clocks to state-of-the-art contemporary navigational instruments. The shop sells many famous Swiss brands: Rolex, Cartier, Patek Philippe, Breitling, Jaeger LeCoultre...

ⓐ Bahnhofstrasse 31 ⓣ 043 344 63 63 ⓦ www.beyer-ch.com
ⓔ info@beyer-ch.com 🕒 14.00–18.00 Mon–Fri ⓝ Tram: 2, 6, 7, 8, 9, 11, 13 (Paradeplatz). Admission charge

Zunfthaus zur Meisen (Guildhall zur Meisen)

The Swiss National Museum's exhibition of porcelain and faience includes a fine collection of delicate 18th-century figurines and dishes from the Zurich porcelain factory in Kilchberg-Schooren. The Zunfthaus zur Meisen, one of the city's most beautiful guild houses, richly embellished with stuccos, is a perfect backdrop for the exquisite displays of baroque table decoration.

ⓐ Münsterhof 20 ⓣ 044 221 28 07 ⓦ www.musee-suisse.ch
ⓛ 10.30–17.00 Tues–Sun ⓝ Tram: 2, 6, 7, 8, 9, 11, 13 (Paradeplatz).
Admission charge

RETAIL THERAPY

Department stores

Globus If you can't find it at Globus, you can probably do
without it; there are seven floors of fashion, jewellery, toiletries,
stationery, and a sensational delicatessen. ⓐ Schweizergasse 11
ⓣ 044 226 60 60 ⓦ www.globus.ch ⓛ 09.00–20.00 Mon–Fri,
09.00–17.00 Sat ⓝ Tram: 6, 7, 11, 13 (Bahnhofstrasse)

Jelmoli Zurich's largest and most popular department store.
ⓐ Seidengasse 1 ⓣ 044 220 44 11 ⓦ www.jelmoli.ch
ⓛ 09.00–20.00 Mon–Fri, 09.00–17.00 Sat ⓝ Tram: 6, 7, 11, 13
(Rennweg)

Fashion

Alprausch A real souvenir alternative to Swiss chocolate, this
young, trendy boutique epitomizes Swiss design with its urban
fashions, snow-wear and accessories. ⓐ Werdmühleplatz 4
ⓣ 043 497 32 00 ⓦ www.alprausch.ch ⓛ 10.00–19.00 Mon–Fri,
10.00–17.00 Sat ⓝ Tram: 6, 7, 11, 13 (Bahnhofstrasse)

Amok One of Zurich's more unusual boutiques, specialising in
skirts for men. ⓐ Ankerstrasse 61 ⓣ 044 291 20 64
ⓦ www.amok.ch ⓛ 09.00–12.15, 13.00–18.30 Mon–Fri,
12.00–16.00 Sat ⓝ Tram: 2, 3 (Bezirksgebäude)

Bally Capitol The world's largest outlet of this famous Swiss institution. ⓐ Bahnhofstrasse 66 ⓣ 044 224 39 39 ⓦ www.bally.ch ⓛ 09.30–19.00 Mon–Tues, 09.30–20.00 Wed–Fri, 09.30–17.00 Sat ⓝ Tram: 6, 7, 11, 13 (Bahnhofstrasse)

Edo Popken In his small boutique at the heart of the banking district, Swiss designer Edo Popken provides shirts and ties for the best-dressed men in town. ⓐ Bärengasse 10 ⓣ 044 221 25 08 ⓦ www.edopopken.ch ⓛ 09.00–18.30 Mon–Fri (until 20.00 Thur), 09.00–17.00 Sat ⓝ Tram: 2, 6, 7, 8, 9, 11, 13 (Paradeplatz)

Grieder This spacious, sophisticated store specialises in prêt-a-porter, haute-couture and exclusive accessories for men and women by such designers as Armani, Kenzo, Gaultier, Fendi and Choo. ⓐ Bahnhofstrasse 30 ⓣ 044 224 36 36 ⓦ www.bongenie-grieder.ch ⓛ 09.00–18.30 Mon–Fri (until 20.00 Thur), 09.30–17.00 Sat ⓝ Tram: 2, 6, 7, 8, 9, 11, 13 (Paradeplatz)

Food

Chäs Vreneli A small cheese shop, renowned beyond the Swiss borders for its selection of regional cheeses. Try the Tilsiter, Appenzeller, Emmental or, for fondue, some Gruyère and Vacherin Fribourgeois. ⓐ Munsterhof 7 ⓣ 044 221 32 81 ⓦ www.chaes-vreneli.ch ⓛ 06.30–18.30 Mon–Fri, 06.30–16.00 Sat ⓝ Tram: 2, 6, 7, 8, 9, 11, 13 (Paradeplatz)

Confiserie Sprüngli Sprüngli is Switzerland's most famous chocolatier, founded in 1836. Still today the world-famous *pralinés*, *truffes du jour*, *Luxembourgerli* (tiny, cream-filled, coloured meringues) and other specialities are lovingly hand-made daily, following traditional recipes. Upstairs is a coffee shop. ⓐ Paradeplatz (Bahnhofstrasse 21) ⓣ 044 224 47 11 ⓦ www.spruengli.ch ⓛ 07.30–18.30 Mon–Fri, 08.00–16.00 Sat ⓝ Tram: 2, 6, 7, 8, 9, 11, 13 (Paradeplatz)

Teuscher This elaborately decorated Altstadt chocolate shop tempts passers-by to stop for a box of speciality hand-made truffles. Try the champagne and orange ones! ⓐ Storchengasse 9 ⓣ 044 211 51 53 ⓦ www.teuscher.com ⓛ 08.00–18.30 Mon–Fri,

● *If you like meringue, you'll love* Luxembourgerli

08.00–17.00 Sat, 16.00–18.00 Sun Ⓝ Tram: 2, 6, 7, 8, 9, 11, 13 (Paradeplatz)

Gifts & toys

Fabric Frontline The exceptional silks here, ranging from ties and scarves to reams of fabric in vivid colours and prints, draw such designers as Lacroix, Givenchy and Vivienne West to this small textile house. ⓐ Ankerstrasse 118 ⓣ 044 241 64 55 ⓦ www.fabricfrontline.ch Ⓛ 10.00–18.30 Mon–Fri, 10.00–17.00 Sat Ⓝ Tram: 8 (Helvetiaplatz)

Franz Carl Weber One of the largest toy shops in Europe and every child's dream, with its impressive window displays and dazzling range of toys for all ages. ⓐ Bahnhofstrasse 62 ⓣ 044 225 7878 ⓦ www.fcw.ch Ⓛ 09.00–18.30 Mon–Fri (until 20.00 Thur), 09.00–17.00 Sat Ⓝ Tram: 6, 7, 11, 13 (Bahnhofstrasse)

Pastorini Spielzeug A magical toy shop, with three floors of imaginative wooden toys, musical instruments, dolls and puppets, crafts and educational games. ⓐ Weinplatz 3 ⓣ 044 228 70 70 ⓦ www.pastorini.ch Ⓛ 13.30–18.30 Mon, 09.30–18.30 Tues–Fri, 09.30–16.00 Sat Ⓝ Tram: 6, 7, 11, 13 (Rennweg)

Schweizer Heimatwerk *The* shop for top-quality contemporary Swiss craftwork, with everything from ceramic kitchenware and glass to jewellery and clothing, woodwork and toys. ⓐ Uraniastrasse 1 ⓣ 044 222 19 55 ⓦ www.heimatwerk.ch Ⓛ 09.00–20.00 Mon–Fri, 08.30–17.00 Sat Ⓝ Tram: 4, 15 (Rudolf-Brun-Brücke)

Sibler This wonderful design shop is brimming with witty yet practical household items and gift ideas. ⓐ Münsterhof 16 ⓣ 044 211 55 50 ⓦ www.sibler-shop.ch ⓛ 10.00–19.00 Mon–Fri, 10.00–17.00 Sat ⓝ Tram: 2, 6, 7, 8, 9, 11, 13 (Paradeplatz)

Spitzenhaus Labor An old-fashioned shop, filled with fine table linens from Bern and Zurich and lace from St Gallen and Appenzell. ⓐ Börsenstrasse 14 ⓣ 044 211 55 76 ⓛ 09.30–12.30, 13.30–18.30 Mon–Fri, 09.30–16.30 Sat ⓝ Tram: 2, 8, 9, 11 (Bürkliplatz)

Watches & jewellery
Bucherer An old favourite for jewellery and watches. Look out for Chopard, Tag Heuer, Rolex and other famous Swiss brands. ⓐ Bahnhofstrasse 50 ⓣ 044 211 26 35 ⓦ www.bucherer.com ⓛ 09.00–19.00 Mon–Fri, 09.00–17.00 Sat ⓝ Tram: 6, 7, 11, 13 (Bahnhofstrasse)

Swatch First launched in 1983, the simple, plastic Swiss-designed Swatch is the most successful wrist-watch of all time. Check out the latest seasonal collections here. ⓐ Bahnhofstrasse 94 ⓣ 044 221 28 66 ⓦ www.swatch.ch ⓛ 09.30–19.00 Mon–Fri, 09.30–17.00 Sat ⓝ Tram: 6, 7, 11, 13 (Bahnhofstrasse)

TAKING A BREAK

Confiserie Sprüngli £ ❶ The most select café in town, overlooking Paradeplatz, full of old-time Zürichers enjoying fine

cakes, chocolates and *pâtisseries*. ⓐ Bahnhofstrasse 21, Am
Paradeplatz ⓣ 044 224 47 31 ⓦ www.confiserie- spruengli.ch
ⓛ 07.30–18.30 Mon–Fri, 08.00–16.00 Sat ⓝ Tram: 2, 6, 7, 8, 9, 11, 13
(Paradeplatz)

Mishio £–££ ❷ Trendy, minimalist noodle bar serving tasty
pan-Asian cuisine to eat in or take away. ⓐ Sihlstrasse 9
ⓣ 044 228 76 76 ⓦ www.mishio.ch ⓛ 06.30–23.00 Mon–Sat
ⓝ Tram: 6, 7, 11, 13 (Rennweg)

Bona Dea ££ ❸ This no-smoking vegetarian buffet restaurant
beside the Hauptbahnhof offers a wide choice of delicious
salads and Asian-influenced dishes. ⓐ Bahnhofplatz 15
ⓣ 044 217 15 15 ⓛ 11.00–14.00, 17.30–23.00 ⓝ Tram: 3, 4, 6, 7, 10, 11,
13, 14 (Bahnhofplatz)

Grieder ££ ❹ A favourite haunt for well-heeled shoppers. Enjoy
a coffee or a light lunch on the tree-shaded rooftop terrace.
ⓐ Bahnhofstrasse 30 ⓣ 044 224 36 36 ⓦ www.bongenie-
grieder.ch ⓛ 09.00–18.30 Mon–Fri (until 20.00 Thur),
09.30–17.00 Sat ⓝ Tram: 2, 6, 7, 8, 9, 11, 13 (Paradeplatz)

Hiltl ££ ❺ Hiltl was Europe's first vegetarian eatery when it
opened in 1898. Today it remains Zurich's top vegetarian
restaurant with an excellent salad bar and superb curries, too.
ⓐ Bleicherweg 5 (Sihlstrasse 28 from spring 2007)
ⓣ 044 227 70 00 ⓦ www.hiltl.ch ⓛ 06.00–24.00 ⓝ Tram: 2, 6, 7,
8, 9, 11, 13 (Paradeplatz)

AFTER DARK

Restaurants

Bierhalle Kropf £ ❻ The 'Kropf', as it is fondly called by locals, serves hearty portions of traditional Zurich cuisine and fine beers in a Bavarian-style beer hall. ⓐ In Gassen 16 ❶ 044 221 18 05 ❶ 11.30–23.30 Mon–Sat ❷ Tram: 2, 6, 7, 8, 9, 11, 13 (Paradeplatz)

Reithalle £ ❼ The former military riding school has been converted into a bar, restaurant, theatre and centre of performing arts. Enjoy a wide variety of tasty, international dishes inside the stables or in the spacious cobblestone courtyard. There's also dancing on Saturday nights from 23.45. ⓐ Theaterhaus Gessnerallee, Gessnerallee 8 ❶ 044 212 70 66 ⓦ www.restaurant-reithalle.ch ❶ 11.00–24.00 Mon–Fri, 18.00–24.00 Sat, 18.00–23.00 Sun ❷ Tram: 3

Zeughauskeller £ ❽ The city's top beer hall, housed in a converted 15th-century arsenal, offers traditional Swiss cuisine (including 15 different kinds of sausage dish) washed down with steins of local beer. Try the metre-long sausage; it's enough for four people! ⓐ Bahnhofstrasse 28a ❶ 044 211 26 90 ⓦ www.zeughauskeller.ch ❶ 11.30–23.00 ❷ Tram: 2, 6, 7, 8, 9, 11, 13 (Paradeplatz)

Contrapunto ££ ❾ Linger over a meal on the pavement terrace at this elegant modern Italian restaurant. ⓐ Waaggasse 5/7 ❶ 044 211 65 25 ❶ 11.30–23.30 ❷ Tram: 2, 6, 7, 8, 9, 11, 13 (Paradeplatz)

Tao's ££–£££ ❿   Join the beautiful people for delicious Euro-Asian cuisine in this sophisticated, modern-Oriental restaurant-cum-lounge bar and candlelit garden. ⓐ Augustinergasse 3 ❶ 044 448 11 22 ⓦ www.taos-lounge.com ❶ 11.30–24.00 Mon–Sat ⓝ Tram: 6, 7, 11, 13 (Rennweg)

Caduff's Wine Loft £££ ⓫   This stylish restaurant boasts more than 2,500 different wines, a tempting Mediterranean menu and the longest bar in town. ⓐ Kanzleistrasse 126 ❶ 044 240 22 55 ⓦ www.wineloft.ch ❶ 11.30–14.00, 17.00–24.00 Mon–Fri, 17.00–24.00 Sat ⓝ Tram: 2, 3 (Kalkbreite); Tram: 8 (Bäckeranlage)

Seidenspinner £££ ⓬   This upmarket restaurant and beautiful garden terrace draws a media and fashion crowd. ⓐ Ankerstrasse 120 ❶ 044 241 07 00 ⓦ www.seidenspinner.ch ❶ 12.00–15.00, 18.00–22.30 Tues–Fri, 18.00–22.30 Sat ⓝ Tram: 8 (Helvetiaplatz)

Zunfthaus der Waage £££ ⓭   Top-notch Swiss cuisine in an exquisite setting within a beautiful 17th-century guildhouse. ⓐ Münsterhof 8 ❶ 044 216 99 66 ⓦ www.zunfthaus-zur-waag.ch ❶ 11.30–14.00, 18.00–22.00 ⓝ Tram: 2, 6, 7, 8, 9, 11, 13 (Paradeplatz)

Bars & clubs
Kaufleuten Rub shoulders with celebrities at one of the most glamorous nightclubs in town. ⓐ Pelikanstrasse 18 ❶ 044 225 33 22 ⓦ www.kaufleuten.com ⓝ Tram: 6, 7, 11, 13 (Rennweg)

Niederdorf & beyond

The picturesque Niederdorf district, on the right bank of the
Limmat river, forms the eastern half of the city's Altstadt and
provides a perfect counterpart to glitzy, glamorous Central
Zurich on the left bank, with its chic shopping streets and
finance houses. Niederdorf has a special, village-like charm with
its hilly, cobbled lanes, medieval houses painted in pastel shades
and historic guildhalls. Its centrepiece is the Grossmünster, a
veritable city landmark with its enormous twin towers. Above
the Altstadt is the university with its grandiose architecture, and
Switzerland's top gallery, the Kunsthaus. To the south there is a
wonderful lakeside walk to Zürichhorn Park, past lidos, boat hire,
cafés, museums and ornamental gardens.

SIGHTS & ATTRACTIONS

Botanischer Garten der Universität Zurich
(Botanic Garden of Zurich University)

The stunning plant collections here provide a botanical world
tour, from alpine roses and Mediterranean herbs to desert
plants and tropical rainforests.

ⓐ Zollikerstrasse 107 ⓣ 044 634 84 61 ⓦ www.bguz.unizh.ch
ⓛ garden 08.00–18.00 Mon–Fri, 08.00–17.00 Sat&Sun;
greenhouse 09.30–16.00 ⓝ Bus: 33, 77 (Botanischer Garten)

Chinagarten Zurich (Zurich China Garden)

This lovely traditional South China garden was a gift from
Zurich's twin town, Kunming. Dedicated to 'the three winter

friends' (pine, bamboo and winter cherry), and with ponds, pagodas, exotic planting and inscriptions and paintings, it is an oasis of calm at Zürichhorn Park.

ⓐ Bellerivestrasse ☏ 044 435 21 11 ⓦ www.chinagarten.ch
🕐 11.00–19.00 mid-Mar–mid-Oct ⓝ Bus: 912, 916 (Chinagarten). Admission charge

Grossmünster (Cathedral)

This imposing Romanesque and Gothic cathedral with its two mighty towers stands proudly on a terrace overlooking the Limmat river. According to legend, it was founded by Charlemagne, whose horse faltered at the graves of three early Christian martyrs, Zurich's patron saints Felix and Regula, and their servant Exuperantius.

In the early 16th century, it was the parish church of Huldrych Zwingli and the birthplace of the Reformation (see page 16). In accordance with Zwingli's beliefs, the interior of the Grossmünster is austere. The choir contains striking red and blue stained-glass windows by Augusto Giacometti, which depict the Christmas story, and there is a Renaissance statue of Charlemagne in the crypt, a copy of which crowns the south tower. The bird's eye views from the top of the tower merit the 187-step climb.

ⓐ Grossmünsterplatz ☏ 044 252 59 49 🕐 cathedral 09.00–18.00 mid-Mar–Oct; 10.00–16.00 Nov–Mar; towers 09.15–17.00 Mon–Sat, 12.30–17.00 Sun, Mar–Oct; 10.00–16.00 Sat&Sun, Nov–Feb (weather permitting) ⓝ Tram: 4. Admission charge for tower

HEADLESS SAINTS!

Zurich's cathedral is dedicated to the city's patron saints, Felix, Regula and Exuperantius, who attempted to convert its citizens to Christianity in the 3rd century. According to legend, the governor of the city made them drink molten lead and plunged them into boiling oil. They still refused to renounce their faith, so they were beheaded. Miraculously, even this didn't stop them. They picked up their heads, carried them to the top of a hill (where the cathedral stands today), dug their own graves and then buried themselves. Zurich's seal still honours these martyrs, portrayed carrying their heads under their arms. Their remains are kept in one of the Grossmünster's chapels.

Niederdorf

The eastern part of Zurich's Altstadt is centred on the Niederdorf , a predominantly car-free, village-like district known to locals as the 'Dörfli', which stretches southwards along the riverside for about a kilometre. With its cobbled alleyways awash with small cafés, bars and boutiques, and its sunny courtyards splashed with medieval fountains, it is one of Zurich's most popular districts. During summer months on Niederdorfstrasse (the main street), the cafés and restaurants spill out onto pavement terraces to create a lively atmosphere.

Ⓝ Tram: 4, 15 (Rathaus or Helmhaus); Tram: 3, 4, 6, 7, 10, 15 (Central); Tram: 3 (Neumarkt)

Utoquai

Join sun-seekers at one of the most popular lakeside lidos, with its smart sun-terrace, bar, restaurant, sauna and massage facilities, and boat hire.

ⓐ Utoquai ① 044 251 61 51 ① 07.00–20.00 mid-May–mid-Sept
Ⓝ Tram: 2, 4 (Kreuzstrasse). Admission charge

Zoo Zurich

The city zoo is more than just an animal park. It focuses on endangered animals and attempts to provide authentic habitats for its more than 360 species of animals from around the globe. It has even recreated a Masoala rainforest in its midst. Young children love the Zoolino petting area.

ⓐ Zürichbergstrasse 221 ① 044 254 35 05 Ⓦ www.zoo.ch
① 09.00–18.00 Mar–Oct (Masoala rainforest from 10.00);
09.00–17.00 Nov–Feb (Masoala rainforest from 10.00)
Ⓝ Tram: 5, 6 (Zoo). Admission charge

△ A typical narrow, cobbled lane, Niederdorf

Zürichsee (Lake Zurich)

One of the city's most pleasurable experiences is to stroll along the east bank of the lake, admire its beautiful scenery by day and by night, and enjoy its many facilities, which range from pedalo hire to steamboat excursions, restaurants, lidos, picnic areas, gardens and even an open-air cinema in summer. Look out for the **Johann Jacobs Museum**, dedicated to coffee (ⓐ Seefeldquai 17 Ⓦ www.johann-jacobs-museum.ch. Admission charge); the attractive **Museum Bellerive**, with its changing exhibitions of applied arts (ⓐ Höschgasse 3 Ⓦ www.museum-bellerive.ch. Admission charge); the **Chinagarten**; and Jean Tinguely's perpetual-motion sculpture '**Heureka**', built for the 1964 National Exhibition. Take a break at one of the cafés or enjoy fresh fish at Fischstube Zürichhorn (see page 92) and, whatever you do, enjoy the tranquillity of the lake away from the frenetic city centre.

CULTURE

Cabaret Voltaire

The Dada art movement was founded here at Cabaret Voltaire almost a hundred years ago in 1916, and was a popular rendezvous for such artists and writers as Hans Arp and Hugo Ball (see pages 14–15). Today it contains a small museum devoted to Dadaism and an arty upstairs café.
ⓐ Spiegelgasse 1 ⓣ 043 268 57 20 Ⓦ www.cabaretvoltaire.ch
Ⓛ museum 13.00–19.00 Tues–Sun; café 11.30–19.00 Tues–Sun
Ⓜ Tram: 4, 15 (Rathaus). Admission charge

E G Bührle Collection

One of the world's most celebrated private art collections, housed in an elegant 19th-century villa. Industrialist Ernst Bührle's paintings include some major old master works, but the focal point is his dazzling French Impressionist collection, with significant works by such artists as Cézanne, Monet, Picasso, Renoir and Van Gogh.

ⓐ Zollikerstrasse 172 ❶ 044 422 00 86 Ⓦ www.buehrle.ch
🕐 14.00–17.00 Tues–Wed, Fri, Sun Ⓝ Tram: 2, 4 (Wildbachstrasse). Admission charge

Heidi-Weber-Haus, Centre Le Corbusier

'A house is a machine for living in' once remarked the celebrated Swiss architect and visual artist Le Corbusier. He created the Heidi-Weber-Haus to represent the culmination of his studies in the fields of architecture, interior design and visual arts, and to serve as a museum of his life and works. The resulting minimalist edifice of glass and steel, with its brightly coloured enamel blocks and umbrella roof, was his last building, completed posthumously in 1967, and reflects his ideological formalism.

ⓐ Hoeschgasse 8 ❶ 044 383 64 70 Ⓦ www.lecorbusier-center.com
🕐 14.00–17.00 Sat & Sun, July–Sept Ⓝ Bus: 912, 916 (Chinagarten). Admission charge

Helmhaus & Wasserkirche (Water Church)

According to legend, the gothic Water Church was constructed on the execution site of Felix and Regula, Zurich's patron saints (see page 82). As with the city's other churches, it was robbed of

its treasures during the Reformation. The adjacent Baroque
Helmhaus has been used as a courtroom and a covered market
over the years. Today it is an imaginative exhibition space for
young artists to showcase contemporary Swiss art.

ⓐ Limmatquai 31 ❶ 044 251 61 77 ⓦ www.helmhaus.org
🕒 10.00–18.00 Tues–Sun Ⓝ Tram: 4, 15 (Helmhaus)

Kunsthaus (Museum of Fine Arts)

The collections in Switzerland's premier gallery span Swiss and
International art from the Middle Ages to the present day, and
contain major loans of Impressionist and Expressionist works.
Newly renovated, the museum counts among the most modern
and sophisticated in Europe, and its audio-guides provide in-
depth information on over 200 artworks by all the big names,
including Rembrandt, Rubens, Tiepolo, Monet, Picasso, Rodin,
Dalí, Lichtenstein and Pollock. Highlights include paintings by
Züricher Post-Reformation artists, 19th- and 20th-century Swiss
art, the Edvard Munch collection (the largest outside Oslo), and
the Swiss-born Alberto Giacometti Foundation.

ⓐ Heimplatz 1 ❶ 044 253 84 84 ⓦ www.kunsthaus.ch
🕒 10.00–21.00 Tues–Thur, 10.00–17.00 Fri–Sun Ⓝ Tram: 3, 5, 8, 9
(Kunsthaus). Admission charge

Museum Schweizer Hotellerie & Tourismus
(Swiss Hostelry & Tourism Museum)

Trace Switzerland's world-famous hospitality and tourism
history through temporary exhibitions in this tiny but
fascinating townhouse museum in Niederdorf.

ⓐ Trittligasse 8 ❶ 044 391 82 78 🕒 14.00–17.00 Wed & Fri,

11.00–17.00 Sat, 11.00–13.00 Sun, May–Dec Ⓝ Tram: 4, 15 (Helmhaus)

Universität (University)

Zurich boasts Switzerland's leading university, the Federal Institute of Technology (ETH), which, over the years, has produced 28 Nobel Prize winners, including Albert Einstein, who especially enjoyed the city views from the Polyterrace, which is open to visitors. The university complex contains several specialist museums, including the Archäologische Sammlung der Universität (Archaeological Collection Ⓦ www.archinst.unizh.ch), the Graphische Sammlung der

🔺 *The Chinagarten Zurich (Zurich China Garden) is an oasis of calm*

ETH (Collection of Prints and Drawings www.gs.ethz.ch) and the Zoologisches Museum der Universität (www.unizh.ch/zoolmus). Tram: 6, 9, 10 (ETH/Universitätsspital)

RETAIL THERAPY

Fashion & design

Andy Jllien Swiss-designed shoes for all occasions from sandals with teetering heels to multi-coloured loafers and jazzy Wellington boots. Torgasse 5–6 044 252 19 11 11.00–18.30 Mon, 09.30–18.30 Tues–Fri (until 19.00 Thur), 09.30–17.00 Sat Tram: 2, 4, 5, 8, 9, 11, 15 (Bellevue)

Neumarkt 17 One of the most extraordinary shops in Zurich, this is a rabbit warren of stylish interior design and modern furnishing. Neumarkt 17 044 254 38 38 www.neumarkt17.ch 09.00–18.30 Tues–Fri, 09.00–16.00 Sat Tram: 3 (Neumarkt)

Food

Schwarzenbach An old-fashioned grocery shop in Niederdorf specializing in 'colonial goods', including teas, coffee, nuts, dried fruit, herbs and spices, oils and chocolates. There is a small café, too. Münstergasse 19 044 261 13 15 08.00–18.30 Tues–Fri, 09.00–17.00 Sat Tram: 4, 15 (Rathaus)

TAKING A BREAK

Altstadt £ ❶ This cool, smoke-free café-bar near the Grossmünster is a popular meeting point for breakfast, coffee, lunch or a relaxed aperitif. ⓐ Kirchgasse 4 ❶ 044 250 53 53 ⓦ www.hotel-altstadt.ch ❶ 07.00–24.00 ❶ Tram: 4, 15 (Helmhaus)

Café Schober £ ❷ A delightful old-fashioned tearoom and Zurich's oldest confectionery, serving delicious coffees, hot chocolate with whipped cream, mouth-watering pastries and chocolates. ⓐ Napfgasse 4 ❶ 044 251 80 60 ❶ 08.00–16.30 Mon–Fri, 08.00–18.30 Sat, 10.00–17.30 Sun ❶ Tram: 4, 15 (Rathaus)

Café Zähringer £ ❸ Popular with students, this bright, atmospheric café serves healthy, organic, mostly vegetarian

● *Schwarzenbach, an old-fashioned Niederdorf grocery shop*

food. ⓐ Zähringerplatz 11 ⓣ 044 252 05 00 ⓛ 18.00–24.00 Mon,
08.00–24.00 Tues–Thur, 08.00–00.30 Fri–Sat, 08.00–24.00 Sun
ⓝ Tram: 4, 15 (Rudolf-Brun-Brücke)

Mövenpick Ice Cream Gallery £ ❹ Treat yourself to a Swiss-
made ice-cream, by the lake, in a bewildering choice of flavours,
including espresso, pistachio, grapefruit, apple, Swiss chocolate…
ⓐ Theaterstrasse 8 ⓣ 043 268 04 20 ⓦ www.moevenpick-
icecream.com ⓛ 11.00–23.00 ⓝ Tram: 2, 4, 5, 8, 9, 11, 15 (Bellevue)

Sternen Grill £ ❺ This sausage stand serves the best fast food
in town. Even local resident Tina Turner queues here for a 'St
Galler Bratwurst mit Gold Burli' (a sausage wrapped in paper, a
bowl of mustard to dunk it in, and a crusty roll). ⓐ Bellevueplatz
ⓛ 11.30–24.00 ⓝ Tram: 2, 4, 5, 8, 9, 11, 15 (Bellevue)

Globus am Bellevue ££ ❻ Eat your way around the world
with light bites and takeaway tapas, panini, noodles, curries
and sushi. ⓐ Theaterstrasse 12 ⓣ 044 266 16 16
ⓦ www.globus.ch ⓛ 07.00–24.00 Mon–Sat, 10.00–22.00 Sun
ⓝ Tram: 2, 4, 5, 8, 9, 11, 15 (Bellevue)

Tibits by Hiltl ££ ❼ Vegetarian fast food for fashionable,
health-conscious Zürichers. Try the sensational buffet.
ⓐ Seefeldstrasse 2 ⓣ 044 260 32 22 ⓦ www.tibits.ch
ⓛ 06.30–24.00 Mon–Fri, 08.00–24.00 Sat, 09.00–24.00 Sun
ⓝ Tram: 2, 4 (Opernhaus)

AFTER DARK

Restaurants

Crazy Cow £ ❽ Hearty Swiss cuisine in a witty restaurant decorated with cartoons, cows, Heidi, Toblerone and other kitsch local memorabilia. Even the menu is in Swiss dialect (with English translations). Try the scrumptuous *rösti* dishes or the Alpen Macaroni. ⓐ Leonhardstrasse 1 ❶ 044 261 40 55 ⓦ www.crazycow.ch ❶ 11.00–23.00 ❶ Tram: 6, 7, 10, 15 (Haldenegg)

Adler's Swiss Chuchi £–££ ❾ Excellent-value fondues and *raclette* dishes in a bright, modern, alpine setting, plus plenty of authentic Swiss specialities for non-cheese-lovers, all washed down with local wines. At the end of the meal, the bill is presented inside a musical box. ⓐ Rosengasse 10 ❶ 044 266 96 96 ⓦ www.hotel-adler.ch ❶ 11.30–23.15 ❶ Tram: 4, 15 (Rudolf-Brun-Brücke)

Blinde Kuh £–££ ❿ As the world's first 'dark restaurant', the hugely popular Blinde Kuh ('Blind Man's Bluff') offers the unique experience of losing your sight for the duration of your meal as you dine in total darkness. No lights are allowed inside; you have to place your watch and mobile phone in a locker before you go in, to ensure total darkness, and even the waiters are blind or partially sighted. ⓐ Mühlebachstrasse 148 ❶ 044 421 50 50 ⓦ www.blindekuh.ch ❶ 18.30–23.00 Mon, 11.30–14.00, 18.30–23.00 Tues–Fri, 18.30–23.00 Sat & Sun ❶ Tram: 2, 4 (Höschgasse)

Bodega Espanola ££ ⓫ This cosy, rustic, first-floor restaurant serves traditional Spanish fare. On the ground floor is a buzzing tapas bar. ⓐ Münstergasse 15 ⓣ 044 251 23 10 ⓛ restaurant 12.00–14.00, 18.00–24.00; tapas bar 10.00–24.00 ⓝ Tram: 4, 15 (Rathaus)

Le Dezaley ££ ⓬ A friendly restaurant specialising in traditional Vaudois dishes, including superb fondues, served in a series of characterful, interconnecting dining rooms and a small courtyard garden in summer. ⓐ Römergasse 7 ⓣ 044 251 61 29 ⓦ www.le-dezaley.ch ⓛ 11.30–14.00, 18.00–24.00 Mon–Sat ⓝ Tram: 4, 15 (Helmhaus)

Fischstube Zürichhorn ££ ⓭ One of the top fish restaurants, with a beautiful terrace beside the lake. ⓐ Bellerivestrasse 160 ⓣ 044 422 25 20 ⓦ www.fischstube.ch ⓛ 09.30–23.30 May–Sept ⓝ Tram: 2, 4

Mère Catherine ££ ⓮ Enjoy Provençal cuisine at this small courtyard restaurant at the heart of Niederdorf. ⓐ Nägelihof 3 ⓣ 044 250 59 40 ⓦ www.commercio.ch ⓛ 11.30–24.00 ⓝ Tram: 4, 15 (Rathaus)

Blaue Ente £££ ⓯ Join Zurich's smart set for light and sophisticated French cooking in a converted ancient water mill on the banks of the lake, which combines old steam machines and giant water wheels with minimalist glass-and-chrome decor. At night the restaurant's lounge converts into a fashionable chill-out bar. ⓐ Seefeldstrasse 223 ⓣ 044 388 68 40

ⓦ www.blaue-ente.ch ⓛ 11.30–00.30 Mon–Sat, 11.30–23.00 Sun
ⓝ Tram: 2, 4 (Wildbachstrasse)

Kronenhalle £££ ⓰ Join Zurich's movers and shakers in the
city's top restaurant and enjoy upmarket Swiss staples in a
traditional, rustic setting, with chandeliers and wood-panelled
walls adorned with original canvases by such luminaries as
Picasso, Chagall, Kandinsky and Matisse. ⓐ Rämistrasse 4
ⓣ 044 262 99 00 ⓦ www.kronenhalle.com ⓛ 12.00–24.00
ⓝ Tram: 2, 4, 5, 8, 9, 11, 15 (Bellevue)

Zunfthaus zum Rüden £££ ⓱ Rich, hearty, Swiss cuisine in a
stunning Gothic riverside guildhall. ⓐ Limmatquai 42
ⓣ 044 261 95 66 ⓦ www.hauszumrueden.ch ⓛ 12.00–15.00,
18.30–24.00 Mon–Fri ⓝ Tram: 4, 15 (Rathaus)

Zunfthaus zur Schmiden £££ ⓲ The 16th-century 'Guildhall of
the Smiths' provides a classy setting for fine Swiss-German
specialities. Try the delicious *Zürcher Geschnetzeltes*.
ⓐ Marktgasse 20 ⓣ 044 250 58 48
ⓦ www.zunfthausschmiden.ch ⓛ 11.00–14.00, 18.00–23.00
Mon–Fri ⓝ Tram: 4, 15 (Rathaus)

Bars & clubs
Ba Ba Lu This trendy post-modern bar in Niederdorf, complete
with DJ and live music, attracts a young, lively crowd.
ⓐ Schmidgasse 6 ⓣ 044 251 9732 ⓝ Tram: 4, 15 (Rudolf-Brun-
Brücke)

Zurich West

The city's former industrial quarter has undergone radical change in the past decade, most noticeably in the once-seedy 'Kreis 5' district around the site of the former Löwenbräu Brewery. It is now the heart of the city's hip scene, a multi-cultural area brimming with trendy bars, restaurant and clubs, and around-the-clock activity. The area is also notable for its inspirational architectural projects, with several old factories converted into living, office and leisure spaces. Shops, galleries and museums – including the Migros Museum and the Zurich Design Museum – focus on the latest trends in contemporary art, while the more traditional Swiss National Museum is among the nation's top museums.

SIGHTS & ATTRACTIONS

Flussbad Obere Letten

One of the trendiest and most popular lidos, where people come for a dip in the canal or a drift downstream in the river, past sundecks, *boules* and beach volley-ball pitches. By night, the right bank of the canal turns into Pier West, an open-air bar with live DJs playing groovy sounds.

ⓐ Lettensteg 10 ⓣ 044 362 92 00 ⓛ 09.00–20.00 mid-May–mid-Sept ⓝ Tram: 4, 13 (Limmatplatz)

Platzspitz

During the 1980s this spacious park behind the Swiss National Museum was sadly known as 'Needle Park', the largest meeting place for drug addicts in Switzerland, and best avoided by city dwellers. In 1993, the area was smartened up and it is now a popular and tranquil retreat stretching along the rivers Limmat and Sihl. It also marks the starting point for river cruises to the lake.

ⓐ Platzspitz ⓝ Tram: 4, 11, 13, 14 (Bahnhofquai)

Puls 5

Puls 5 is a trendy new lifestyle complex at the heart of the former industrial district of Zurich West, beside the Schiffbau. This architecturally innovative development contains at its heart a concrete-wrapped former Giessereihalle (foundry), together with a supermarket, fitness centre, apartments, shops, bars and restaurants. Still in its infancy, Puls 5 is fast becoming one of the hip addresses in town. Watch this space!

ⓐ Puls 5, Turbinenplatz ⓝ Tram: 4, 13 (Escher-Wyss-Platz)

ⓞ *Schweizerisches Landesmuseum is a Swiss cultural landmark*

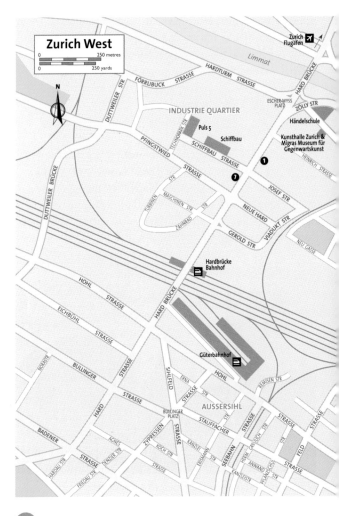

Zurich West

0   250 metres
0   250 yards

N

Limmat

Zürich
Flugafen

HARD BRÜCKE

HARDTURM STRASSE

FÖRRLIBUCK STRASSE

DUTTWEILER STR

ESCHER-WYSS
PLATZ

ZOLLY STR

INDUSTRIE QUARTIER

Händelschule

Puls 5

TECHNOPARK STR

PFINGSTWIED

SCHIFFBAU STRASSE

Schiffbau

Kunsthalle Zurich &
Migras Museum für
Gegenwartskunst

HEINRICH STRASSE

STRASSE

DUTTWEILER BRÜCKE

TURBINEN STR

MASCHINEN STR

ZAHNRAD

JOSEF STR

NEUE HARD

VIADUKT STR

GEROLD STR

NEU GASSE

Hardbrücke
Bahnhof

HOHL

STRASSE

EICHBÜHL

STRASSE

HARD BRÜCKE

Güterbahnhof

HOHL

VERBUSEN STR

NORA STR

BULLINGER

HARD

STRASSE

STRASSE

SIHLFELD

ERNA

STR

STRASSE

AUSSERSIHL

STR

STRASSE

BADENER

STRASSE

AGNES

ZYPRESSEN

BULLINGER
PLATZ

STRASSE

KOCH STR

STAUFFACHER

ERISMANN STR

KANZLEI

SEEBAHN

STRASSE

HOH DREILICHT STR

ANWAND

WELANCHTUS

STRASSE

FELD

STR

STRASSE

HARPAUI STR

FRIEDAU STR

GENZER STR

STRASSE

KANZLI STR

Schiffbau

This striking 19th-century industrial building was once used for building ships and lake-cruisers. Today the ramshackle red-brick factory forms the heart of an avant-garde arts complex, containing a top-notch restaurant, bar, jazz club and a second stage for Zurich's best-known theatre, the Schauspielhaus.

ⓐ Schiffbaustrasse 4 (off Hardstrasse) Ⓝ Tram: 4, 13 (Escher-Wyss-Platz)

CULTURE

Kunsthalle Zurich

One of two major museums in the converted Löwenbräu Brewery, the Kunsthalle focuses on the city's contemporary art scene with frequently changing exhibitions to showcase the work of up-and-coming internationally significant new artists.

ⓐ Limmatstrasse 270 (second floor) ⓣ 044 272 15 15
ⓦ www.kunsthallezurich.ch ⓛ 12.00–18.00 Tues, Wed & Fri, 12.00–20.00 Thur, 11.00–17.00 Sat & Sun Ⓝ Tram: 4, 13 (Dammweg). Admission charge

Migros Museum für Gegenwartskunst
(Migros Museum for Contemporary Art)

The bright, lofty white rooms on the first floor of the former Löwenbräu Brewery building provide the perfect setting for modern art displays. The permanent collection contains around 1,300 artworks by 700 international artists, which rotate alongside temporary exhibitions.

ⓐ Limmatstrasse 270 ⓣ 044 277 20 50

Ⓦ www.migrosmuseum.ch Ⓛ 12.00–18.00 Tues, Wed & Fri,
12.00–20.00 Thur, 11.00–17.00 Sat & Sun Ⓝ Tram: 4, 13
(Dammweg). Admission charge

Museum für Gestaltung Zurich (Zurich Design Museum)

This top-notch museum features changing exhibitions on
various aspects of design, architecture, photography, visual
communications and multi-media, covering everything from
'Swiss-made' consumer goods to 'Gay Chic' and 'Take-away'
(designs for eating on the move). The Plakatraum (Poster
Collection) across the road within Zurich's Design School
(ⓐ Limmatstrasse 55) draws on an extensive archive of vintage
posters for its temporary exhibitions.

ⓐ Ausstellungsstrasse 60 Ⓣ 043 446 67 67 Ⓦ www.museum-
gestaltung.ch Ⓛ 10.00–20.00 Tues–Thur, 10.00–17.00 Fri–Sun
Ⓝ Tram: 4, 13 (Museum für Gestaltung). Admission charge

Schweizerisches Landesmuseum (Swiss National Museum)

One of Zurich's top museums, it contains the world's largest
collection of Swiss historical and cultural artefacts. It
documents Swiss civilisation from pre-history to the modern
age in over 100 rooms, with special emphasis on pre-history and
the Middle Ages. Highlights include children's toys, silverware,
Renaissance globes, regional costumes and an impressive
collection of artefacts from each of the country's cantons.

ⓐ Museumsstrasse 2 Ⓣ 044 218 65 11 Ⓦ www.musee-suisse.ch
Ⓛ 10.00–17.00 Tues–Sun Ⓝ Tram: 4, 11, 13, 14 (Bahnhofquai).
Admission charge

RETAIL THERAPY

Freitag Shop Zurich Surely the most unusual shop in town, the Freitag tower is a veritable mini-skyscraper, built out of 17 freight containers. It houses over 1,600 individually designed bags, wallets and accessories in all colours, shapes and sizes.
ⓐ Geroldstrasse 17 ⓣ 043 366 95 20 ⓦ www.freitag.ch
ⓛ 11.00–19.30 Mon–Fri, 11.00–17.00 Sat ⓝ S-Bahn: Hardbrücke;
Bus: 72, 33 (Pfingstweidstrasse)

◐ *Freitag Shop Zurich, home of recycled chic*

TAKING A BREAK

Back & Bräu £ ❶ 'Bake & Brew' is something of a Swiss institution; a micro-brewery-cum-bar-cum-restaurant, which serves tasty savoury pies and pasties accompanied by delicious seasonal house beers. ⓐ Heinrichstrasse 267 ❶ 044 271 1030 ⓦ www.backundbrau.ch ❶ 09.00–24.00 Mon–Thur, 09.00–01.00 Fri & Sat, 11.00–24.00 Sun ⓝ Tram: 4, 13 (Escher-Wyss-Platz)

Lily's Stomach Supply £ ❷ A trendy noodle bar serving delicious pan-Asian cuisine at long, communal tables. Ideal for those on a budget. Try the Pakistani curry or the Japanese *yaki soba* noodles, washed down with beers from around the world. ⓐ Langstrasse 197 ❶ 044 440 18 85 ⓦ www.lilys.ch ❶ 11.00–24.00 Mon–Thur, 11.00–01.00 Fri & Sat, 15.00–24.00 Sun ⓝ Tram: 4, 13 (Limmatplatz)

Swiss Museum Café £ ❸ Enjoy coffee and cake or a light lunch snack at this jazzy, minimalist café in the Landesmuseum. ⓐ Museumsstrasse 2 ❶ 044 218 65 11 ❶ 10.00–17.00 Tues–Sun ⓝ Tram: 4, 11, 13, 14 (Bahnhofquai)

AFTER DARK

Restaurants
Il Posito Solito £ ❹ This old-fashioned, family-run Italian restaurant serves some of the best pizzas in town. ⓐ Gasometerstrasse 26 ❶ 044 272 62 92 ⓝ Tram: 4, 13 (Limmatplatz)

Josef ££ ❺ Join the local 'in' crowd at this small but popular restaurant, with its stylish interior, exellent wine list and simple, Swiss-Italian menu. ⓐ Gasometerstrasse 24 ❶ 044 271 65 95 ⓛ 11.30–14.00, 18.30–23.00 Mon–Fri, 18.30–23.00 Sat & Sun ⓝ Tram: 4, 13 (Limmatplatz)

El Parador ££ ❻ Try the delicious prawns in garlic, paella or a variety of other authentic specialities in this highly regarded Spanish restaurant. ⓐ Luisenstrasse 43 (cnr Heinrichstrasse) ❶ 043 366 88 85 ⓦ www.elparador.ch ⓛ 11.30–14.30, 18.00–24.00 Mon–Fri ⓝ Tram: 4, 13 (Limmatplatz)

LaSalle £££ ❼ The unusual setting and artful modern European cuisine draws Zurich's chic set to this sophisticated, minimalist restaurant. ⓐ Schiffbaustrasse 4 ❶ 044 258 70 71 ⓦ www.lasalle-restaurant.ch ⓛ 11.00–24.00 Mon & Tues, 11.00–01.00 Wed & Thur, 11.00–02.00 Fri, 17.00–02.00 Sat, 17.00–24.00 Sun ⓝ Tram: 4, 13

Sala of Tokyo £££ ❽ One of Switzerland's best Japanese restaurants. Booking essential. ⓐ Limmatstrasse 29 ❶ 044 271 52 90 ⓦ www.sala-of-tokyo.ch ⓛ 11.45–14.00, 18.00–22.45 Tues–Fri, 18.00–22.45 Sat ⓝ Tram: 4, 11, 13, 14 (Bahnhofquai)

Bars & clubs
Most of the district's nightlife is focused on trendy Limmatstrasse, with a cluster of bars and clubs around Escher-Wyss Platz too.

◗ *Elaborate window detail, Lucerne*

Zürichsee (Lake Zurich)

Lake Zurich offers an enormous choice of short excursions. Near the city, its shores are dominated by grassy parks, lakeside promenades and early 20th-century mansions. Further afield, picturesque villages such as Rapperswil and Küsnacht punctuate the shoreline, flanked by lush, green countryside and gentle hills – a veritable walker's paradise. Even the lake itself offers a wide variety of activities, including sailing, pleasure-boat cruising and swimming.

GETTING THERE

The region is easy to explore by boat, on foot or on wheels.

By boat

The options are many: a day cruise to Rapperswil for lunch, museums and shopping; a morning cruise from Thalwil to Küsnacht for a lazy lakeside lunch; or escape the crowds and enjoy a relaxing stroll on the island of Ufenau. The Zürichsee Schifffahrtsgesellschaft (ⓐ Mythenquai 333 ⓣ 044 487 13 33 ⓦ www.zsg.ch) offers a variety of excursions from two-hour mini-cruises to full day outings. During summer months ZSG ferries stop at every lakeside town.

By bike

The lake region is also ideal for cyclists. You can either pedal round the lake (along the 'Seestrasse'), or ride a section of National Bike Route Number 9; called the 'Route des Lacs', this is one of nine national bicycle touring routes, and it takes keen cyclists right across Switzerland from Lake Constance to Lake Geneva. Bikes are available for rental at train stations in Rapperswil, Uznach, Ziegelbrücke, Forch and the Zurich Hauptbahnhof. ⓦ www.rentabike.ch ⓣ 0900 300 300

By S-Bahn

The train lines run the length of both shores, offering an easy, scenic journey to such destinations as Rapperswil and Küsnacht. Depending on the time you wish to travel, you may consider purchasing a 9-Uhr Tagespass (9 o'clock Daypass), valid after 09.00 Monday to Friday and all day Saturday and Sunday.

◄ *Sailing on the Zürichsee*

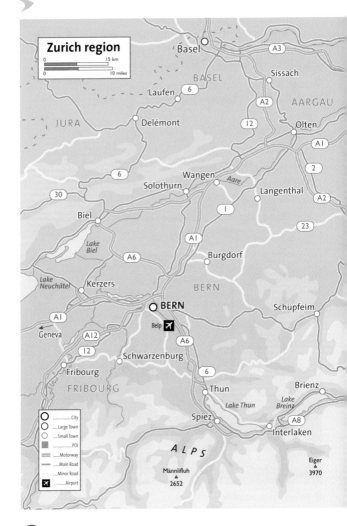

Zurich region

0 — 15 km
0 — 10 miles

Basel

Sissach

BASEL

Laufen 6

AARGAU

JURA

Delémont

12

Olten

A3

A2

A1

6

Wangen

Aare

2

30

Solothurn

Langenthal

A2

Biel

1

23

Lake
Biel

A6

A1

Lake
Neuchâtel

Kerzers

Burgdorf

BERN

Schüpfeim

A1

Geneva

A12

Belp ✈

A6

Schwarzenburg

12

Fribourg

FRIBOURG

6

Thun

Brienz

Lake
Thun

Lake
Breinz

Spiez

Interlaken

A8

ALPS

Männlifluh
2652

Eiger
▲
3970

○ City
○ Large Town
○ Small Town
◼ POI
▬ Motorway
▬ Main Road
▬ Minor Road
✈ Airport

SIGHTS & ATTRACTIONS

Alpamare

Europe's largest indoor water-park, with ten thrilling water-slides, fun indoor and outdoor pools and wellness attractions too, including Switzerland's only iodine brine pool, thermal pools, whirlpools and saunas.

ⓐ Gwattstrasse 12, Pfäffikon ⓣ 055 415 15 15 ⓦ www.alpamare.ch
ⓛ 10.00–22.00 Tues–Thur, 10.00–23.00 Fri, 09.00–23.00 Sat, 09.00–22.00 Sun & Mon ⓝ S-Bahn: S2, S8 (Pfäffikon). Admission charge

Knies Kinderzoo (Knies Children's Zoo)

Children adore this well-known children's zoo, where they can pet, stroke and feed many of the 300-plus animals here, marvel at the performing sea lions, and ride elephants, camels and ponies.

ⓐ Oberseestrasse 41, Rapperswil ⓣ 055 220 67 60
ⓦ www.knieskinderzoo.ch ⓛ 09.00–18.00 Mon–Sat, 09.00–19.00 Sun, mid-Mar–Oct ⓝ S-Bahn: S5, S7 (Rapperswil). Admission charge

Küsnacht

The hamlet of Küsnacht basks on the Goldküste ('Gold Coast'), the fashionable, eastern side of the lake, named after its golden afternoon sunshine and glorious sunsets. Since 1986 it has been home to American pop star, Tina Turner. The main appeal of Küsnacht is its celebrated restaurant. It also marks the start of the Küsnachter Tobel, a beautiful 7-km (4½-mile) pathway through shady forest, with excellent lake vistas en route. The lido is popular during summer months.

Ⓝ S-Bahn: S6, S7, S16

Rapperswil

This atmospheric lakeside town is sometimes called the 'City of Roses', due to its numerous rose gardens. One of the most delightful gardens is designed for the blind, with highly fragranced specimens and information in brail. Another lies within the 16th-century Cappuchin monastery. Other highlights include the Knies Children's Zoo (see page 108), the Circus Museum and an impressive medieval castle that contains a small museum devoted to Switzerland's Polish community (Ⓦ www.muzeum-polskie.org Ⓛ 13.00–17.00 Apr–Oct). Explore the narrow streets and alleys of the medieval old town and be sure to pause a while in Fischmarktplatz, the most picturesque square – open to the lake and fringed with café terraces and a small marina.

Ⓐ Rapperswil Zürichsee Tourismus, Fischmarktplatz 1 Ⓣ 0848 811 500 Ⓛ 10.00–17.00 Apr–Oct; 13.00–17.00 Nov–Mar Ⓝ hourly boat from Bürkliplatz (duration two hours); S-Bahn: S5, S7 (Rapperswil)

Stäfa

The main attraction of this unremarkable town is that it is the lake's largest wine-producing community, located at the foot of the Pfannenstiel (pan handle) – the main vine-growing area of the canton – near the stunning 27.6-km (17-mile) Pfannenstiel Panoramaweg (panoramic footpath Ⓦ www.zpp.ch). Two wine paths also start in Stäfa, with information panels providing wine lovers with valuable facts and figures about the grapes and wine culture of the lake.

S-Bahn: S7

Ufenau

Escape the city hubbub and visit the tranquil island of Ufenau during your lake cruise. The largest of two islands in the lake and measuring just 750 m by 200 m (2,460 ft by 656 ft), it is a perfect place to relax and enjoy nature. Stroll round the perimeter, sunbathe, visit the St Peter and St Paul Church with its 2nd-century Gallo-Romanic temple, or enjoy a meal at the self-service restaurant (🕒 Mar–Oct). Regrettably, swimming on the island is prohibited as it is a protected nature reserve.

🌐 www.ufenau.ch 🚊 Boat (see 🌐 www.zsg.ch)

🔺 Lake Zurich's 'Gold Coast'

Wädenswil

Winter is the best time to visit Wädenswil, when the natural outdoor ice skating rink beside the lake is open.
❶ 043 477 91 51 ⓦ www.eisbahnwaedi.ch ⓒ check the website for rink's opening times Ⓝ S-Bahn: S2, S8 (Wädenswil). Admission charge

CULTURE

Bergwerkmuseum Käpfnach (Coal Mining Museum)

Housed within an 18th-century coal storeroom, this unusual museum provides a rare glimpse into the history of coal mining and especially the miners' day-to-day lifestyle.
ⓐ Bergwerkstrasse 27, Horgen ❶ 044 725 39 35
ⓦ www.horgen.net ⓒ 13.00–16.30 Sat, Apr–Nov Ⓝ S-Bahn: S2, S8. Admission charge

Circus Museum Rapperswil

A fascinating insight into the history of Rapperswil's famous Knie family and its National Circus, its animal training and circus stunts, through colourful exhibits of ancient costumes, old posters, rare props and video films. Children especially enjoy trying on the old costumes in the 'kids' corner'.
ⓐ Fischmarktplatz 1, Rapperswil ❶ 055 220 57 57 ⓒ 10.00–17.00 Apr–Oct; 13.00–17.00 Nov–Mar Ⓝ S-Bahn: S5, S7 (Rapperswil). Admission charge

FURTHER AFIELD

Atzmännig

A trip to Atzmännig makes a fun day out as it is home to Switzerland's most exciting summer toboggan run. At 700 m (2,297 ft) long, its sharp bends, steep gradients and tunnels provide an adrenaline rush for all the family. During summer months there are wonderful country walks. In winter, the snowy slopes are popular with skiers and snowboarders.

ⓐ Sportbahnen Atzmännig, Goldingen ❶ 055 284 64 34 ⓦ www.atzmaennig.ch ❶ 10.00–11.45, 13.15–17.00 Mon–Fri, 08.30–17.15 Sat & Sun, Apr–May; 09.00–11.45, 13.15–17.15 Mon–Fri, 08.30–11.45, 13.15–17.15 Sat & Sun, June–Sept; 08.00–11.45, 13.15–17.00 Mon–Fri, Oct; 09.00–16.00 Mon–Fri, 08.30–16.30 Sat & Sun, mid-Nov–Mar ❷ Train: Atzmännig

Einsiedeln

Set in picture-postcard scenery less than an hour by train south of Lake Zurich, the town of Einsiedeln is the nation's most important pilgrimage site, drawing a quarter of a million devotees annually to its vast Kloster, the Baroque Benedictine Abbey. Its lavish interior contains a much-revered Black Madonna, and there are daily guided tours, which provide fascinating insight into the life of the monks and the history of the abbey.

Einsiedeln Tourismus ⓐ Hauptstrasse 85, Einsiedeln ❶ 055 418 44 88 ⓦ ww.einsiedeln.ch
Kloster Einsiedeln ⓐ Benzigerstrasse, Einsiedeln ❶ 055 418 61 11 ⓦ www.kloster-einsiedeln.ch ❶ 05.30–20.30 ❷ Train: Einsiedeln (change at Wädenswil)

Hoch Ybrig

Zurich's nearest ski resort is easily accessible by train.
In summer, hikers enjoy the idyllic landscape in the foothills
of the Alps. In winter, it becomes a winter sports paradise,
offering both downhill and cross-country skiing. The children's
ski school is one of the best in Switzerland.

Ferien & Sportzentrum Hoch Ybrig ⓐ Waagtalstrasse 127,
Hoch Ybrig ⓣ 055 414 60 60 ⓦ www.hoch-ybrig.ch or
www.ybrig.ch ⓝ Train: to Einsiedeln, then bus

RETAIL THERAPY

Lindt & Sprüngli Chocolate Factory, Kilchberg

There is a distinct fragrance of chocolate in the town of
Kilchberg, thanks to the presence of the vast Lindt & Sprüngli
Chocolate Factory. Founded in 1836, Sprüngli remains
Switzerland's most famous chocolatier. Its exquisite truffles and
pralines are regarded by many as the ultimate in Swiss
chocolate, freshly hand-made daily. ⓐ Seestrasse 204, Kilchberg
ⓣ 044 716 22 33 ⓦ www.lindt.com ⓛ museum temporarily closed
for renovation; shop 10.00–19.00 Mon–Thur, 10.00–17.00 Fri
ⓝ S-Bahn: S1, S8 (Kilchberg)

TAKING A BREAK

Marsala ££ A smart, modern restaurant serving tasty Italian and
Sicilian dishes near the harbour. ⓐ Seequai/Marktgasse 21,
Rapperswil ⓣ 055 211 22 24 ⓦ www.marsala.ch ⓛ 11.00–14.00,
18.00–24.00 Mon–Fri, 11.00–24.00 Sat & Sun

Schützenhaus ££ A small, popular fish restaurant with beautiful views and alfresco dining, right on the lake. ⓐ Seestrasse 48, Stäfa ⓣ 044 926 13 58 ⓦ www.schutzenhaus.com ⓛ 10.00–24.00 Thur–Mon

AFTER DARK

Restaurants
Petermann's Kunststuben £££ Reputedly the best restaurant in Switzerland. Michelin-starred Horst Petermann's inventive cuisine is served with elegance and artistic flair in an intimate dining room. ⓐ Seestrasse 160, Küsnacht ⓣ 044 910 07 15 ⓦ www.kunststuben.com ⓛ 12.00–14.00, 19.00–21.00 Tues–Sat ⓝ S-Bahn: S6, S7, S16 (Küsnacht)

Schloss Rapperswil £££ Rapperswil's top restaurant, located within the castle, and best-known for its sensational fish and seafood dishes. ⓣ 055 210 18 28 ⓦ www.schloss-restaurant.ch ⓛ 11.30–23.30 Tues–Sat, 11.30–15.00 Sun

ACCOMMODATION

Camping Lützelau £ An idyllic campsite on the tiny island of Lützelau with barbecue and picnic areas, and a small restaurant. ⓐ Lützelau ⓦ www.luetzelau.ch ⓛ May–Sept ⓝ Island taxi boat: from Rapperswil

Jakob £ A popular choice at the heart of the old town, with 20 simple but stylish rooms, a classic bistro, trendy bar and beautiful vaulted wine cellar. ⓐ Hauptplatz 11, Rapperswil ⓣ 055 220 00 50 ⓦ www.jakob-hotel.ch

Hirschen-am-See ££ A friendly, country-style guesthouse on the lake, in the small village of Meilen, with two restaurants and panoramic views. ⓐ Seestrasse 856, Meilen ⓣ 044 925 05 00 ⓦ www.hirschen-meilen.ch

Sonne ££ A romantic hotel in a beautiful location on the shore of the lake, with fine dining, fine art (paintings and sculptures by such artists as Tinguely and Warhol) and its very own beer garden and pier. ⓐ Seestrasse 120, Küsnacht ⓣ 044 914 18 18 ⓦ www.sonne.ch

● *Zürichers flock to the lake at weekends*

Lucerne (Luzern)

The city of Lucerne (Luzern in German) is every bit as picturesque as the postcards promise. With its remarkable blend of lakes, mountains, history, culture, folklore and architecture, this charming medieval town in central Switzerland has it all. Little wonder it is a tourist magnet.

Lucerne is located on the northern edge of Lake Lucerne (Vierwaldstättersee) at the foot of majestic Mount Pilatus, and is surrounded by spectacular alpine scenery steeped in the history of William Tell and the formation of the Swiss

�â–² *The iconic Kapellbrücke*

Confederation. The old quarter of town is located on the edge of the lake, and brims with charm and character. Its picturesque streets are dotted with historical monuments, fortifications and churches. The spacious riverbank promenades are ideal for strolling, and the breath-taking countryside is celebrated for its walks, panoramas, folklore and sports.

GETTING THERE

It takes just 50 minutes to reach Lucerne by train from the Zurich Hauptbahnhof (with departures every half hour). For further details of transport, sightseeing or accommodation, contact the Tourist Office:

Luzern Tourismus ⓐ Bahnhofstrasse 3 ⓣ 041 227 17 17 ⓦ www.luzern.org ⓔ luzern@luzern.org

SIGHTS & ATTRACTIONS

Kapellbrücke (Chapel Bridge)

Europe's oldest covered wooden footbridge, spanning the Reuss river, is very much a symbol of Lucerne and the most photographed monument in Switzerland. Following a fire in 1993, it has undergone a major restoration project, including the reproduction of many of its remarkable Renaissance wall paintings.

Löwendenkmal (Lion Monument)

This world-famous monument – 'the dying Lion of Lucerne' – was carved into the sandstone cliff above the town in 1821 to commemorate the heroic deaths of Swiss mercenaries who died in Paris in 1792 trying to save the life of Marie Antoinette. Mark Twain described it as 'the saddest and most moving piece of rock in the world'.

Mt Pilatus

The ascent of Mt Pilatus (2,132 m/6,993 ft), the giant, mystic mountain looming over Lucerne, is one of the most popular excursions in Switzerland. Until the 17th century, people were forbidden to climb it because locals feared that Pontius Pilate's ghost would bring about the downfall of Lucerne. According to legend, his body was brought here by the devil and his spirit haunts the summit.

Queen Victoria reached the top in 1868 on the back of a mule. Nowadays, transportation is easier. Travel by nostalgic lake steamer from Lucerne to Alpnachstad and then with the world's steepest cogwheel railway, at a gradient of 48° (summer months only). Restaurants, a large sun terrace and dazzling 360° views over the Alps as far as Italy await you at the summit. Then travel via panoramic gondola and cable-car (open all year) down to Kriens for the bus back to Lucerne.

ⓐ Pilatus-Bahnen, Schlossweg 1, Kriens ⓣ 041 329 11 11
ⓦ www.pilatus.com

Mt Rigi

Lucerne's second major viewpoint (after Pilatus), and probably the most famous mountain view in Switzerland, Mt Rigi is called the 'island mountain' as it appears to be surrounded by the waters of lakes Lucerne, Zug and Lauerz. To reach the summit, take a boat from Lucerne to Vitznau, then a cogwheel train to Rigi-Kulm, from where it is a 200-m (656-ft) walk to the summit. There are hiking trails all over the mountain, including several easy routes part-way down to Rigi Kaltbad, where you can either pick up the cogwheel train or return by cable-car to Weggis.

Museggmauer (Musegg Wall)

Walk along the ramparts of the medieval city wall for magnificent views over Lucerne's rooftops to the lake and mountains beyond. The main section of the walk is from Wachtturm to the Zytturm, with the oldest clock in Lucerne, which bizarrely chimes one minute before all the others in town.

🕐 08.00–19.00 Easter–Oct. Admission charge

⬤ *The summit of Mt Pilatus affords awesome views*

Vierwaldstättersee (Lake Lucerne, Lake of the Four Cantons)

The Vierwaldstättersee is one of the most beautiful lakes in Europe, situated at the meeting point of four cantons (Lucerne, Uri, Unterwalden and Schwyz) with fjords that reach finger-like into the mountains. Its clear blue waters entice visitors for a swim or a trip on the nostalgic lake steamers to the various quaint villages dotted along its shores, including the idyllic villages of Gersau, Vitnau and Weggis, which form the 'Innerschweizer Riviera' on the sunny, eastern shore of Lake Lucerne.

The surrounding chocolate-box scenery is Switzerland at its scenic best, with steep, tree-lined cliffs, lush alpine meadows, dense forests and snow-peaked mountains. Not only is this the heart of William Tell country, it is also where the seeds of the Swiss Confederation were sown. It is a walkers'

THE SWISS PATH

Der Weg der Schweiz ('The Swiss Path') is a special 37-km (23-mile) walkers' path around the southernmost part of Lake Lucerne (called Urnersee), designed in 1991 to celebrate the 700 years of the Swiss Confederation. With sensational vistas, plenty of picnic areas and easy access by bus or boat from Lucerne, the walk can be done in various stages. Each section of the walk represents the individual cantons of Switzerland in the order that they joined the Confederation. The length of each canton's stretch represents the number of people living in that canton.

paradise, with numerous well-signposted trails, and cable-cars and mountain railways for easy access to the upper slopes. There are also some excellent cycle trails. Ask the Tourist Office for details:

Schifffahrtsgesellschaft des Vierwaldstättersees

ⓐ Werftestrasse 5 ⓣ 041 367 67 67 ⓦ www.lakelucerne.ch

CULTURE

Kunstmuseum Luzern (Lucerne Art Museum)

Housed in the futuristic KKL Luzern building (see page 125), the Art Museum alternates selections from its permanent collection of Swiss 19th- and 20th-century art with temporary exhibitions of avant-garde contemporary art. Worth a visit for the building alone.

ⓐ KKL Level K, Europaplatz 1 ⓣ 041 226 78 00
ⓦ www.kunstmuseumluzern.ch ⓛ 10.00–17.00 Tues–Sun (until 20.00 Wed). Admission charge

Picasso Museum

If you're expecting Picasso canvases here, you'll be disappointed. There are only a handful of ceramics and sketches. However, there is a fascinating and revealing portrayal of the man through almost 200 photographs (by David Douglas Duncan) illustrating the last 17 years of the artist's life spent with his family in the south of France.

ⓐ Furrengasse 21 ⓣ 041 410 35 33 ⓛ 10.00–18.00 Apr–Oct; 11.00–17.00 Nov–Mar. Admission charge

Sammlung Rosengart (Rosengart Collection)

An acclaimed art museum containing more than 200 works by Cézanne, Chagall, Klee, Picasso, Matisse, Miró, Monet and others, from the private collection of Lucerne art dealer Angela Rosengart.

ⓐ Pilatusstrasse 10 ⓣ 041 220 16 60 ⓦ www.rosengart.ch
ⓛ 10.00–18.00 Apr–Oct; 11.00–17.00 Nov–Mar. Admission charge

Verkehrshaus der Schweiz (Swiss Transport Museum)

This impressive museum pays homage to Switzerland's fascinating history of transport, telecommunications and tourism. Children love the exhibits, which include over 60 locomotives, 50 motorbikes and every other type of transport imaginable, from dugout to spaceship. Space travel is simulated in the Planetarium, and there's even an IMAX cinema showing vivid documentary films on a giant wrap-around 3-D screen.

ⓐ Lidostrasse 5 ⓣ 041 370 44 44 ⓦ www.verkehrshaus.org
ⓛ 09.00–18.00 Apr–Oct; 10.00–17.00 Nov–Mar. Admission charge

RETAIL THERAPY

Bucherer The head office and largest branch of the leading Swiss watch and jewellery retailer, with more than 4,000 items for every taste and budget. ⓐ Schwanenplatz 5 ⓣ 041 369 77 00 ⓛ 08.30–19.30 Mon–Sat (until 21.00 Thur), 16.00–18.00 Sun

Carl Studer Vinothek Come here for expert advice and tastings of fine Swiss wines. ⓐ Langensandstrasse 7 ⓣ 041 360 45 89

Ⓦ www.studer-vinothek.ch Ⓛ 10.00–13.00, 14.00–18.30 Tues–Fri, 10.00–16.00 Sat

Claudia Krebser Locally designed fashions for men and women in a stylish, old-town boutique. Ⓐ Kauffmannweg 12 Ⓣ 041 210 77 23 Ⓦ www.claudiakrebser.com Ⓛ 14.00–18.30 Mon, 09.00–12.30, 14.00–18.30 Tues–Fri, 10.00–16.00 Sat

Conditorei Heini Scrumptuous cakes and pâtisseries, including chocolate cows and 'Luzern Raindrops' (cherry liqueur-filled chocolate drops). Ⓐ Löwenplatz 9 Ⓣ 041 412 20 20 Ⓦ www.heini.ch Ⓛ 06.30–17.00 Mon–Sat, 09.00–18.00 Sun

Luzerner Wochenmarkt The sights, colours and fragrances of the market are a veritable feast for the senses. Ⓐ river quays Bahnhofstrasse & Jesuitenplatz Ⓦ www.luzerner-wochenmarkt.ch Ⓛ Tues & Sat

TAKING A BREAK

Grottino 13/13 £ There's no menu in this atmospheric bistro, just a delicious set menu of simple Italo-Swiss cuisine. Ⓐ Industriestrasse 7 Ⓣ 041 361 13 13 Ⓛ 11.30–14.00, 18.00–00.30 Mon–Fri

Kostgeberei £ Tasty organic cuisine in a simple yet stylish setting. Lunchtimes only. Excellent for vegetarians. Ⓐ Ulmenstrasse 14 Ⓣ 041 360 34 13 Ⓦ www.kostgeberei.ch Ⓛ 12.00–14.00 Tues–Fri

AFTER DARK

Restaurants

Taube £–££ Hearty home-cooking in a rustic setting and the perfect place to sample local dishes. ⓐ Burgerstrasse 3 ⓣ 041 210 07 47 ⓦ www.taube-luzern.ch ⓛ 12.00–14.00, 18.00–22.30 Tues–Sat

◑ *A twilight drink by the River Ruess*

Bodu ££ Paris meets Lucerne at this classic brasserie, with excellent river views and regional French cuisine. ⓐ Kornmarkt 5 ⓣ 041 410 01 77 ⓛ 11.30–23.20 Mon–Sat, 11.30–23.00 Sun

Jasper £££ Inventive Swiss cuisine accompanied by avant-garde decor and dazzling lake views. ⓐ Haldenstrasse 10 ⓣ 041 416 16 16 ⓦ www.palace-luzern.com ⓛ 12.00–14.00, 19.00–22.00

Bars
Pravda The hippest dance club in town, with excellent DJs. ⓐ Pilatusstrasse 29 ⓣ 041 226 88 88 ⓦ www.pravda.ch

Seeburg Lounge & Sunset Bar A suave cocktail lounge for the beautiful people of Lucerne, with a midnight snack bar to keep you going into the early hours. The Sunset Bar is the largest open-air bar in town, right on the lake. ⓐ Seeburgstrasse 51–63 ⓣ 041 375 55 55 ⓦ www.hotelseeburg.ch

Concert venues
Kultur & Kongresszentrum Luzern (Lucerne Culture & Conference Centre) The stunning 'KKL' is an international masterpiece of modern architecture, created by French architect Jean Nouvel, with its roof jutting out far over its floor area and housing an art museum (see page 121) and concert hall with near-perfect acoustics. It is the venue of Lucerne's celebrated International Festival of Music during summer. ⓐ Europaplatz 1 ⓣ 041 226 70 70 ⓦ www.kkl-luzern.ch

ACCOMMODATION

Backpackers Lucerne £ A clean, cheap and friendly hostel by the lake, with family rooms, and also bikes and rollerblades for rent.
ⓐ Alpenquai 42 ⓣ 041 360 04 02 ⓦ www.backpackerslucerne.ch

Magic £–££ Fun and quirky, each room here has a different theme, from Swiss chalet to Aladdin and even pirates.
ⓐ Brandgässli 1 ⓣ 041 417 12 20 ⓦ www.magic-hotel.ch

Montana ££–£££ An opulent art deco hotel on a hill (reached by its own funicular), with breathtaking views across the lake and city to Pilatus. ⓐ Adligenswilerstrasse 22 ⓣ 041 419 00 00 ⓦ www.hotel-montana.ch

The Hotel £££ An ultra-modern boutique hotel in an old town house, designed by Jean Nouvel (of KKL fame, see pages 121 and 125). In each matt-black suite, a gigantic film scene adorns the ceiling. ⓐ Sempacherstarsse 14 ⓣ 041 226 86 86 ⓦ www.the-hotel.ch

◗ *Steamer on Lake Lucerne*

Directory

GETTING THERE
By air
Zurich's Kloten Airport (Ⓦ www.zurich-airport.com) is Switzerland's largest international airport and one of the busiest in Europe, serviced by over 100 different airlines, 75 of which offer scheduled services. Swiss International Air Lines, the national airline, is the main operator of scheduled flights to Switzerland from the UK and Europe, followed by British Airways, Lufthansa and Air France. Flights from the UK take 1½–2 hours to reach Zurich.

Information and online reservations can be made through the airlines' websites:

Air France Ⓦ www.airfrance.ch
American Airlines Ⓦ www.americanairlines.ch
British Airways Ⓦ www.britishairways.com
Delta Ⓦ www.delta.com
Lufthansa Ⓦ www.lufthansa.ch
Swiss Ⓦ www.swiss.com

Many people are aware that air travel emits CO_2, which contributes to climate change. You may be interested in the possibility of lessening the environmental impact of your flight through the charity Climate Care, which offsets your CO_2 by funding environmental projects around the world. Visit Ⓦ www.climatecare.org

By road

It is a long drive from the UK to Zurich, around 700 km
(435 miles) from London. The usual route by car is through
Belgium or the Netherlands and then through Germany. An
alternative route is through France, but tolls are payable on the
French motorways. Before you enter Switzerland, you need to
purchase a *vignette* (annual motorway tax, see page 54).

Coach travel is a reasonably priced option, with discounts for
under 25s, OAPs and those with disabilities. The journey from
London Victoria takes around 18 hours. Contact Eurolines for
further information: **Eurolines** Ⓦ www.eurolines.com

By rail

It's easy to travel from London to Zurich by train and it takes just
12 hours. Take the Eurostar to Paris via the Channel Tunnel, then
a high-speed TGV train from Paris to Zurich. Contact Eurostar or
Rail Europe for further information. For train times and fares
within Switzerland see the Swiss Federal Railways website.
Eurostar Ⓦ www.eurostar.com

TRAVEL INSURANCE

It is important to take out adequate personal travel
insurance for your city break, covering medical expenses,
theft, loss, repatriation, personal liability and cancellation.
If you are travelling in your own vehicle, you should also
ensure that you have the appropriate insurance, and
remember to pack the relevant insurance documents and
your driving licence.

Rail Europe Ⓦ www.raileurope.com
Swiss Federal Railways Ⓦ www.sbb.ch

ENTRY FORMALITIES

Citizens of the UK, Republic of Ireland, other EU countries, the USA, Canada, Australia, New Zealand and South Africa are all permitted to enter Switzerland with a valid passport. A visa is required only if the duration of the stay is more than 90 days.

Visitors to Switzerland from Europe are entitled to bring 200 cigarettes, 50 cigars or 250 g of pipe tobacco. Visitors from non-European countries may import twice as much. The allowance for alcohol is the same for everyone: 1 litre of spirits and 2 litres of wine.

MONEY

The currency in Switzerland is the Swiss franc (CHF), which is made up of 100 centimes (also called Rappen/centesimi in German/Italian-speaking regions). Notes are available in denominations of 10, 20, 50, 100, 500 and 1000 francs, and coins are minted as 5, 10, 20 and 50 centimes, and also 1, 2 and 5 francs.

Fittingly, there are plenty of banks to choose from in Zurich. You can change money at banks, as well as at bureaux de change booths at the airport and the train station. ATMs are also common, accessible 24 hours a day, and have multi-lingual instructions. Most international bank or credit cards are accepted if you wish to withdraw Swiss francs, provided you know your PIN. Credit cards are widely accepted throughout the city, especially EuroCard and MasterCard.

HEALTH, SAFETY & CRIME

Zurich's water is safe to drink, as is the water from most of the city's fountains. The city's food should present no health risk to travellers.

The quality of health care in Zurich is generally very high. There is no free state health service in Switzerland, but thanks to a reciprocal agreement, citizens of the UK and other EU countries are entitled to reduced-cost, sometimes free, medical treatment on presentation of a valid European Health Insurance Card (EHIC – apply online at ⓦ www.dh.gov.uk/travellers). On top of this, private medical insurance is still advised and is essential for all non-EU visitors.

Zurich is essentially a safe city but, although crime rates are relatively low, it is advisable to take commonsense precautions against petty crime: don't carry excess cash; use the hotel safe for valuable goods; beware of pickpockets in crowded places; and stick to well-lit, populated areas by night. See 'Emergencies' section for police details and listings (pages 138–139).

OPENING HOURS

Museum and gallery opening times vary. Many open on Sunday and close for at least one day a week, often on Monday.

Most shops open 09.30–18.30 Mon–Fri, and 08.30–16.00 or 17.00 Sat. Many stay open for late-night shopping until 20.00 Thur.

Restaurants usually open 12.00–14.00 and 18.00–22.00, and are at their busiest around 20.30.

Bank hours vary, but are generally 08.30–16.30 Mon–Fri (until 18.00 Thur).

TOILETS

Public toilets charging CHF 1 or CHF 2 are generally pretty clean and can be found at all central points, including the Hauptbahnhof (also with showering facilities), Bellevueplatz and Paradeplatz. They are open daily, usually 05.00–24.00.

CHILDREN

There are plenty of attractions to keep children amused in the city, including some wonderful toy shops. Restaurants and cafés will generally be happy to cater for children and some offer special menus or portions. Nappies, baby food and formula milk can be bought in supermarkets.

Some of the most appealing attractions for children include:

- **Alpamare** A fantastic water park, with indoor and outdoor pools and crazy slides (see page 108).

- **Biking** Older children will enjoy cycling around the city or along the lake shore. You can hire a bike for free from Zürirollt (see page 58).

- **Chocolate shops** Chocolate shops abound in the city and are always great for treats! Sprüngli and Teuscher count among the best, with branches throughout the city.

- **Circus** Zurich is circus-crazy, with various shows throughout the year. The best is undoubtedly the world-renowned Swiss National Circus Knie (Mar–Apr), with its famous elephant, horse and seal acts. ⓦ www.knie.ch

- **Ice skating** The Dolder Ice Skating Rink is a great place for a family outing. There are even mini 'push-penguins' to help the little ones along. ⓐ Adlisbergstrasse 36 🕐 09.00–22.00 Mon–Sat, 09.00–17.30 Sun Ⓥ Tram: 3 (Römerhof), then take the Dolderbahn to Eisbahn station

- **Lake Zurich** Whether you take a traditional steamboat excursion, hire a bicycle or a pedalo, picnic on the shore or simply swim at one of the lidos, there's plenty to keep all the family amused in or around the lake.

- **Playgrounds** Some of the best playgrounds can be found in Fortunagasse (just beneath Lindenhof), beside the China Garden at Zürichhorn, and on the corner of Spiegelgasse and Untere Zäune in Niederdorf.

⬥ Children will find it hard to resist the charms of a furry friend

- **Uetliberg** Take the kids up Uetliberg for some fresh mountain air and exercise. Older children in particular will enjoy the 'Planets Trail', a two-hour hike from Uetliberg to Felsenegg, with models of the planets on a scale of 1:1 billion.

- **Zinnfiguren Museum Zurich (Pewter Figure Museum Zurich)** With 40,000 fascinating pewter figures, including children's toys and brightly painted tin soldiers, this place is ideal for older children. ⓐ Obere Zäune 19 ⓣ 044 262 57 20 ⓦ www.zinnfigurenmuseum.ch. Admission charge

- **Zoo Zurich** There's fun for all the family at this world-class zoo. Older children adore the Masoala Rainforest while the Zoolino petting area is especially popular with toddlers (see page 83).

- **Spielzeugmuseum (Zurich Toy Museum)** A fascinating collection of antique toys from all over Europe. ⓐ Fortunagasse 15 ⓣ 044 211 93 05 ⓛ 14.00–17.00 Mon–Fri, 13.00–16.00 Sat

COMMUNICATIONS
Phones
The city's trendy new public phones (ⓦ www.swisscom.com) are easy to spot – stylish glass-and-granite cylinders that glow pink at night. They are also straightforward to use, with instructions in English. Basically, lift the handset, insert payment then dial the number. They take major credit cards (Visa, MasterCard, Amex, Diners Club and JCB) and the following coins: CHF 1, CHF 2 and CHF 5 plus 10, 20 and 50 centimes.

TELEPHONING SWITZERLAND
To phone Switzerland from abroad, dial your international access code (usually 00), then the national code for Switzerland (41), followed by the area code for Zurich, minus the initial 0 (44) and the local number.

TELEPHONING ABROAD
To phone home from Zurich, dial the outgoing code (00), followed by the relevant country code (see below), area code (minus the initial 0 if there is one) and local number.

Australia 43
New Zealand 64
Republic of Ireland 353
South Africa 27
UK 44
USA & Canada 1

National enquiries 1811
International operator 1811

For reverse charge/collect calls to USA, Canada, Japan, UK and Australia and world-wide calls with a credit card, dial 0800 265 532, wait for the prompt and dial 1 for English or 0 for the operator.

Postal services
There are three ways to send your mail from Switzerland: Urgent (for same-day or next-day international deliveries); Airmail (Europe) and Airmail (rest of world).

Sihlpost (Main Post Office) ⓐ Kasernenstrasse 95–97
🕐 06.30–22.30 Mon–Fri, 06.30–20.00 Sat, 10.00–22.30 Sun
Swiss Post ⓦ www.swisspost.ch

Internet

For those who would rather email, many hotels now offer internet and WLAN access, and there are internet cafés around the city too, although these tend to be quite expensive. Most public phone boxes have an electronic phonebook, which enables you to send short emails worldwide.
Internet Café Urania ⓐ Uraniastrasse 3 ⓣ 044 210 33 11
ⓦ www.cafe.ch 🕐 07.00–23.00 Mon–Fri, 08.00–23.00 Sat, 10.00–22.00 Sun

ELECTRICITY

The electricity supply in Zurich is 220 V, 50 Hz. Swiss sockets are generally recessed, and plugs are round, flat or hexagonally shaped with two pins. British and US appliances need a plug adaptor, and North American appliances also need a transformer.

TRAVELLERS WITH DISABILITIES

Switzerland is well prepared to receive travellers with disabilities and the facilities are generally of a high standard. The following are useful resources:
Behinderten Transport Zurich (Zurich Transport for the Physically Disabled) provides a 24-hour bus service for passengers in wheelchairs. ⓣ 044 444 22 11 ⓦ www.btz.ch
Disabled Persons Transport Advisory Committee (UK)
ⓦ www.dptac.gov.uk/door-to-door

Trip Scope (UK) 🕿 0845 758 641 🌐 www.tripscope.org.uk
Mobility International Switzerland (MIS) 🕿 062 206 88 35
🌐 www.mis-ch.ch
Switzerland Tourism publishes a useful hotel guide specifically
for visitors with disabilities. 🌐 www.myswitzerland.com

FURTHER INFORMATION

Zurich's Tourist Information Office is located at the
Hauptbahnhof (main train station) and is a useful source for
maps, attractions and event information and any other queries
you have about the city and the rest of Switzerland. It also offers
a hotel reservation service. ⓐ Hauptbahnhof 🕿 044 215 40 00
🖷 044 215 40 44 🌐 www.zuerich.com
ⓔ information@zuerich.com 🕓 08.30–19.00 Mon–Sat,
09.00–18.30 Sun, Nov–Apr; 08.00–20.30 Mon–Sat, 08.30–18.30
Sun, May–Oct

BACKGROUND READING

There are surprisingly few books solely about Zurich, and very
few Swiss authors have been translated into English.

Novels featuring the city:
Patricia Highsmith, *Small g: A Summer Idyll*, 1995. Lives and loves
in a gay bar in Zurich.
Robert Ludlum, *The Bourne Identity*, 1980. A thriller set in
Marseille, Zurich and Paris of the 1970s.
Michael Pye, *The Pieces from Berlin*, 2003. Wartime reflections,
set in Zurich.

Emergencies

EMERGENCY NUMBERS
Police ☎ 117
Fire ☎ 118
Ambulance ☎ 144
Crisis line ☎ 143
24-hour doctor (Ärtzefon) ☎ 044 421 21 21

Medical services

Should you become seriously ill, lists of local doctors, dentists and hospitals can be found in telephone directories or by contacting your consulate, who have lists of English-speaking practitioners. Alternatively, ask your hotel reception to help or, in a real emergency, dial 144.

Zurich has one of the best health care systems in the world with modern, well-equipped hospitals and superb nursing care. If you have a valid European Health Insurance Card (EHIC, see page 131) you will be entitled to cheaper, sometimes free, medical treatment. However, dental care, except emergency accident treatment, is not available free of charge.

24-hour pharmacy, Bellevue Apotheke ⓐ Theaterstrasse 14 ☎ 044 266 62 22 ⓦ www.bellevue-apotheke.com ⓝ Tram: 2, 4, 5, 8, 9, 11, 15 (Bellevue)

Kinderspital The specialist children's hospital. ⓐ Steinwiesstrasse 75 ☎ 044 266 71 11 ⓝ Tram: 3, 8 (Hottingerplatz)

Universitätspital (University Hospital) The main city hospital. It has over 1,000 beds and an accident centre. It is also one of

the world's leading heart-surgery centres. ⓐ Rämistrasse 100
ⓣ 044 255 11 11 Ⓜ Tram: 6, 9, 10 (ETH/Universitätsspital)
University of Zurich Dental Clinic ⓐ Plattenstrasse 11 ⓣ 044 634
33 11 Ⓜ Tram: 5, 6 (Platte)

Police
Kantonspolizei Zurich (Cantonal Police Station)
ⓐ Hauptbahnhof ⓣ 044 247 22 11
Stadtpolizei Zurich (City Police Station) ⓐ Bahnhofquai 3
ⓣ 044 411 71 17 (24-hour service)

Embassies & consulates
Australia ⓐ Chemins des Fins 2, Geneva ⓣ 022 799 91 00
Canada ⓐ Kirchenfeldstrasse 88, Bern ⓣ 031 357 32 00
New Zealand ⓐ Chemins des Fins 2, Geneva ⓣ 022 929 03 50
Republic of Ireland ⓐ Claridenstrasse 25, Zurich ⓣ 044 289 25 15
South Africa ⓐ Alpenstrasse 29, Bern ⓣ 031 350 13 13
UK ⓐ Hegibachstrasse 47, Zurich ⓣ 044 383 65 60
US ⓐ Dufourstrasse 101, Zurich ⓣ 044 422 25 66

EMERGENCY PHRASES

Help! Hilfe! *Heelfe!*   **Fire!** Feuer! *Foyer!*   **Stop!** Halt! *Halt!*

Call an ambulance/a doctor/the police/the fire service!
Rufen Sie bitte einen Krankenwagen/einen Arzt/die Polizei/
die Feuerwehr!
*Roofen zee bitter inen krankenvaagen/inen artst/dee
politsye/dee foyervair!*